The Stud
Assign
Disse
Survi guide

by George Ajuga

Answering the Question Behind the Question!

The tricks and secrets to getting high marks for your assignments and dissertation time-after-time

About the Author

George Ajuga, BA (Hons), MBA, was the assignments director at Lecturers Direct (a leading UK student assignment consultancy group) for over ten years and, in his time there, assisted thousands of students in compiling their respective assignments and dissertations irrespective of length, nature or academic level. He has also been (and continues to be) a private consultant, lecturer and assignment advisor to hundreds of students all over the country assisting them to obtain top marks, constantly, in their endeavours. In working for the company and assisting students within a private capacity, he gained a deep insight and invaluable experience into the secrets and techniques into writing and compiling assignments.

George learned a great deal during his time with Lecturers Direct and now sets out to share those learnings in a systematic way. The secret to getting consistent 'A' grades in your assignments is down to one thing - technique. Having mastered this technique, the author now shares his knowledge with you thus demystify the writing of assignments and dissertations so that they will no longer be so terrifying and harrowing for you when you set about preparing to compile and write these academic works.

Having interacted with a hundreds of students in various universities all over the country, as well as having spoken with numerous lecturers, George Ajuga felt it appropriate to write this document. By looking through the Contents page of this guide, you will notice its no-nonsense 'bottom-up' approach. After all, as a student, you will have come to realise that an assignment does not begin (as some books would have you believe) at writing the assignment's introduction. Far from it. Instead, it starts from the moment you receive the assignment in your lecture or tutorial. George's guidance begins from that point.

Contents

Introduction

 Rationale for writing this practical guide

All too often, I find that most books professing to help students in compiling all manner of academic assignments only touch on certain key areas of the reader's needs. Consequently, they often only serve to leave the student more confused than before.

This practical step-by-step guide adopts a different approach and, as I hope you'll agree, the right approach. Having carried out a rigorous consultation with the people who really matter (i.e. students themselves), I have adopted what I would call a 'bottom-up' approach and, in doing so, have taken matters from the moment you are handed the assignment question by the lecturer. This in turn should enable you to identify, immediately and easily, with the guidance offered in this book.

This practical guide neither bombards you with big words nor colourful graphics - remembering that old adage: "All that glitters is not gold". My comprehensive research has told me that students don't care for unnecessary verbiage nor for line-upon-line of irrelevant information. All students care about is getting excellent results. This practical guide tells you how to do just that without all the unnecessary bells and whistles.

By looking through the 'Contents' page of this guide, you will notice its no-nonsense 'bottom-up' approach. After all, as a student, you will have come to realise that an assignment does not begin (as some books would have you believe) at the time of writing the assignment's introduction. Far from it. Instead, it starts from the moment the student receives the assignment in the lecture or tutorial; so, we take it from there.

And what do I know about it? Well, having worked for a well-known company which specialises in helping university students all over the UK compile all manners of academic assignments ranging from reports to essays, textual analysis to dissertations, I gained a deep insight and invaluable experience into the secrets and techniques which contribute to the successful completion of an assignment.

In my years working for that company, I was the Assignment Director, which entailed overseeing and supervising all academic assignments irrespective of length, nature or academic level. During my time in their employ - all twelve years of it - I learned a great deal and so I set out to share those learnings in a systematic way. I want to demystify the writing of assignments and dissertations, so that they will no longer seem so terrifying and harrowing for those preparing to compile and write those academic works.

Like most things, writing good quality assignments and dissertations, time-after-time, is not down to luck. Instead, it is 100% technique. If you can master the technique, you're nearly all the way there to obtaining the coveted first class degree.

The emphasis is decidedly on producing winning assignments and dissertations. This guide does not attempt to bog you down with the unnecessary detail but instead goes to the heart of the matter and guides you as if I were by your side from the moment you receive the assignment or dissertation notice. Being in college or university, you would have (or are about to, if you are a first year student) invested considerable time, energy and money in this endeavour and you (and your parents) want the return to reflect that significant investment.

 Structure of the guide

In structuring the guidelines, after the "Introduction", the guide is divided into four main parts the first of which takes the student through the assignment-writing process from the moment the student is handed the assignment in class by his or her lecturer. What happens next? The guide takes it from there.

The second part is a brief description of report writing whilst part three steers the student through the dissertation process from the moment the student is notified by the university that they will be expected to compile a dissertation in their final year as part of the third year modules.

Although the exact time differs between universities, having spoken to a number of students from different universities around the country, the normal time is just before the (2nd year) students break up for the long Summer break and before their exams. They are notified that they will be expected to submit a proposal on a topic of their choice (that must relate to their respective degree) and have it approved by the lecturer or more to the point, their allocated/chosen supervisor. This guide takes it from the moment they are notified of this academic requirement.

In a similar manner the fourth part of the guide is dedicated to assisting postgraduate students in completing their final dissertation project successfully.

As the old adage goes: "knowledge is power". I would also add to that by stating that "knowledge and technique are power". One without the other, within the confinements of compiling academic assignments, is useless but having both can be awesome for any student intent on consistently getting high marks.

Parts one to four have thus described the techniques to be applied in compiling all manner of assignments, reports and dissertations. Consequently, part five outlines all the recommended sources from which to acquire the best knowledge. In maintaining the concept of not confusing students and of keeping things simple, this section lists the author's recommended research sources by degree. The list comprises various research institutes, libraries, websites and search engines that will be needed to acquire the research material to compile your successful assignment/dissertation.

Throughout the text can be found related and important areas such as key words within essays. What do they mean? How does one go about interpreting the question? You'd be surprised at how many students get this wrong. Instead of specifically addressing what the lecturer wants, they opt to address what they *feel* the lecturer wants and in the process often lose valuable marks in answering the question in the wrong manner. Having used this guide, you'll never make that mistake again.

Assignments - Typical problems encountered

In my 12 years with the aforementioned company, I can honestly say that any assignments we helped to compile never achieved less than a mark of 65% (B+). This was quite a feat when you consider that we never attended a specific student's tutorial, as well as the fact that, in deciding a particular student's assignment mark, a lecturer takes into account a whole lot more than just the quality of the piece of work. Other things he or she takes into account include the student's attendance record, his or her contribution in tutorials, their enthusiasm for the subject, how friendly they are with the student (and other things I wouldn't like to mention!).

Having interacted with hundreds of students in various universities all over the country, as well as having spoken with numerous lecturers, I felt it appropriate to write this book. It encapsulates all the various and typical problems that students normally encounter when, for instance, writing assignments; some of these problems are outlined in the panel on the following page:

Assignments - Some Typical Problems & Questions

What is the lecturer looking for in this assignment?

What are the key areas to include in order to maximise my marks?

Where is the best place to obtain quality yet affordable (and, where possible, free) research material?

What is the best way to interpret and reword the question so as to help me fully understand it?

I don't know how to begin writing the essay?

What do certain key words mean in the assignment's instructions? Key words such as: 'Account for'; 'Analyse'; 'Argue'; 'Discuss'; 'Comment on'; 'Compare'; 'Criticise'; 'Contrast'; 'Evaluate'; 'Assess'; 'Outline'; 'Describe'; 'Identify'; 'Illustrate'; 'Justify'; 'Prove' - to mention but a few.

How do I reference the essay the right way to maximise marks?

What should I include in the bibliography to maximise marks?

What is the best way to obtain the research? (Students must not confuse this with "Where is the best place to obtain the research?").

Having obtained the research, how do I utilise the information and data to ensure maximum marks?

I have to hand in my assignment tomorrow and I haven't even started - what can I do as I need to pass to keep up my grades?

And many, many more!

4 ► Dissertations - Typical problems encountered

And then there are 'dissertations'! Writing dissertations is an entirely different ball game. In most universities, dissertations normally count for at least two modules towards the student's final degree so you'd better make it good, as you only get one shot at it. Getting a good mark could be the difference between a 2:1 (60-69%) and a 1:1 (70-100%).

Dissertations normally range anything between 6,000 words and 12,000 words for undergraduate students and 15,000 to 20,000+ words for postgraduate students. The main differences between a dissertation and assignment (apart from the amount of words to be written) are that, firstly, a dissertation often needs to be more academic with top quality (usually Harvard style) referencing and, secondly, it usually requires what is known as a 'literature review'. It also demands a significant input of primary research to support (or refute) any theories, hypotheses, arguments, etc. being expressed in the dissertation. There are other key areas that need to be included in the dissertation and all these are discussed in detail in this guide.

Like most things, writing a quality academic dissertation is 10% luck and 90% technique. Technique encapsulates various areas such as research (primary and secondary) quality, structuring and presentation of the dissertation, referencing, etc. Don't forget that when your lecturer (or in the case of dissertations - supervisor) is marking your dissertation, he or she is likely to use a marking criteria, which normally includes areas such as structure, introduction, literature review, executive summary, primary research and subsequent analysis, quality and feasibility of findings and recommendations and conclusion.

Other important considerations affecting the marking are the paper's grammar and presentation - after all, what use is a dissertation if the marker can't understand the English and what's the use if the dissertation is structured and presented in an incoherent manner?

Typical problems I frequently encountered from students are:

Dissertations - Some Typical Problems & Questions

What subject should I pick to write about?

What is a 'literature review' and what is the best way to write one for my dissertation?

What is the quick and effective way to carry out and include primary research in my dissertation?

I've already picked a subject but, having started the dissertation, I am having severe difficulties writing more words? How can I resolve this problem?

My supervisor is not flexible in letting me decide on the content for my dissertation.

How can I go about obtaining quality primary research and, having obtained it, how can I best implement and analyse it so as to include it in my dissertation?

I've requested primary research by way of interviews and/or questionnaires to be answered from a company but they've turned me down or not responded. My problem is that I must include primary research in my dissertation. What shall I do? Is there another way?

What is the best way to structure the dissertation to maximise my marks?

What key areas will I need to include in it to stand out from everyone else and, in the process, really impress my Project Supervisor?

How do I go about making feasible and logical recommendations (where applicable) for my dissertation? Is there a quick source of good and relevant recommendations to include in the dissertation?

What do I include in my bibliography? How long does it need to be?

And many, many more!

Above are only some of the problems which I have frequently encountered in my years of helping students to compile assignments and dissertations. As a result, it inspired me to write this practical guide not only to pose the typical problems that students often face but, more importantly, how best to solve those problems and proceed to write a quality assignment/dissertation thus progressing to a good degree.

5 Recommendations

This book is a *must* for any student attending university or college (or, indeed, those intending to progress to university/college) and for all those who consider themselves serious and ambitious. It is a no-nonsense, no-waffle book avoiding all the useless jargon contained in many academic books. Instead, it outlines real life problems that students often encounter and in the process offers practical, implementable and - most importantly - simplistic solutions that all students can understand and relate to. What is more, it is officially recommended and endorsed by the No.1 student website *just4students.com*. Unlike other practical guides, this one has been priced sensibly so as to be affordable to students with very limited budgets. When you get it, all we ask is that you don't tell anyone else you've got it - let them buy their own copy!

The pace of higher education is changing rapidly. The idea of lecturers spending lots of time with a few students, or students reading lots of readily available books or journals, and of students then receiving individual tutorials or participating in small seminar groups is perhaps wonderful but, with notable exceptions, an impossibility.

Over the years, student numbers have increased much faster than the number of lecturers. This means bigger classes, fewer seminars and tutorials and less detailed feedback about assessment by academic staff. Consequently, every student will need this practical guide to see him or her through university/college.

Assignments

1 ▶ Receiving the assignment in a lecture or tutorial

You've just received the assignment in class

This is usually where the whole process begins. We commence our scenario at the end of the lecture or tutorial, where the lecturer has just handed you the assignment question. What do you do next? What you don't do is simply put the question sheet in your folder and leave the class. What you do is to question the lecturer - either in the class or, preferably (if you want to be really smart), after the class when everyone has gone - asking if he or she has any tips for you. That is to say: "Excuse me Sir/Madam, what key things do you want to see in this?" (Perhaps the old adage is appropriate here: "Why wonder? It costs nothing to ask.").

This approach has various advantages. For example, it shows the lecturer that you are serious and you take his or her subject very seriously. Secondly, it flatters him/her in that you value their professional opinion. Thirdly, it gives you an advantage over your fellow students in that you have a head start. Lastly, even if you don't write the essay very well, the lecturer will remember your eagerness and keenness to perform well in his/her essay and, hopefully, show mercy and generosity when marking your paper.

Remember, although what you write counts towards a lot, what the lecturer also perceives about you as a student (and, believe me, they secretly do) also counts.

An assignment with a choice of questions

In certain cases, the assignment sheet may contain a number of questions from which you need to make a choice. If you are given a choice, ensure you read each title carefully and make sure you really understand each meaning.

Remember that the longest question is not necessarily the most difficult - nor is the shortest the easiest. Remember also that you are representing yourself and need to make the best possible impression. A bad choice could cause you lots of extra work, a good deal of frustration and damage your chances of success.

Don't share your advantage

Having received some tips, what do you do next? One thing you don't do is run and tell your best friend who happens to be in the same class as you - he or she may tell someone else and before you know it, your advantage has been eroded and the whole objective defeated.

Remember, if everyone has the same tips, the chances are that everyone will include the same key points in their respective essay. With this being the case, when the lecturer marks the essays, if he or she notices that each essay contains the same key points, all they'll do is award everyone more or less the same marks.

One thing that gets you extra marks is by impressing the lecturer and you do this by standing out from the crowd. So, unless you are Snow White or the Pope, make sure you keep your mouth shut having obtained an important, early advantage.

 Understanding and interpreting the question

With the lecturer's tips in your head or better still jotted down on a piece of paper and a permanent grin on your face, the next stage is to interpret and understand the question. Many students often underestimate the importance of this stage but if you don't fully understand the question, how can you be in a position to know what research material you will need to tackle it? For example, let's take a typical essay question:

"A cultural diverse work force equals competitive advantage for the global firm." Discuss.

Now, the above question can mean any number of things but one thing is for sure, before you can go about obtaining research to begin answering it, you will first of all need to understand the question fully.

As mentioned earlier, the first step would have been to get tips from the lecturer. Well, he or she would have told you that, in answering the above question, you would need to look at cultural diversity within an organisational setting.

The same question can now be reworded the following way:

"In this era of globalisation, in employing a work force that is culturally diverse (i.e. from various cultural backgrounds) does such an employment strategy necessarily give the firm a competitive advantage over its rivals?"

Note that we haven't looked at the key word in the question, which is "*Discuss*". We'll come to that later.

Having reworded the question to a manner which suits you - particularly "you", because you are going to write it so you have to be comfortable with the question. After all, you wouldn't get behind the wheel of a car, and adopt the driving-seat position of the previous driver would you? As you are going to drive the car, you'll need to adjust the seat to a position you feel the most comfortable. The car's occupants don't care in what position your seat is as long as they get to their destination. Likewise, the lecturer doesn't care how you reword the question as long as it is answered correctly.

The next stage lies in understanding the meaning of "*Discuss*". This is extremely important as getting this wrong can drastically tip the balance of the whole assignment. It is essential that you understand exactly what you are required to do. Following is a selection, in alphabetical order, of some of the more common key words (including "*Discuss*") and what they mean:

 Instructions defined

Account for - Here, the lecturer is asking you to give the reason for something or give evidence to support a particular statement. This must not be confused with '*give an account of*'.

Analyse - Here, the lecturer is asking you to examine and explain the relationships between various parts of the topic at hand.

Argue - Here, the lecturer is asking you to employ the use of evidence to either prove or disprove a particular point of view. The student will need to set it out logically and, in the process, attempt to disprove other points of view.

Assess - Here, the lecturer is asking you to employ the use of evidence to estimate the value or importance of something.

Comment on - Unfortunately, a very commonly used 'coverall' phrase, which is rather vague. The lecturer probably really wants you to analyse or assess. You may also be required to give your view on a particular issue backed up by evidence. Any tips obtained from the lecturer would really help here for reasons of clarity.

Compare - Here, the lecturer is asking you to concentrate on those aspects, which two or more things have in common - although it would be wise to deal with any differences as well.

Contrast - Here, the lecturer is asking you to concentrate on any differences - but do mention any similarities where possible.

Criticise - Here, the lecturer is asking you to try and find fault with the value of something or the truth of a statement. You must state the evidence upon which you base your judgment and as a result, comprehensive referencing (preferably Harvard Style) will be needed here.

Define - Here, the lecturer is asking to state precisely the meaning of something with no unnecessary waffle.

Describe - Here, the lecturer is asking you to relate what something looks (or sounds, feels, smells) like, how a sequence of events happened or what are the main characteristics of a topic.

Discuss - In relation to the example question set above and, in general, when asked to '*discuss*' a particular statement, the lecturer is in effect asking you to outline the pros and cons of the statement and, in the process, give your own justified view. Additionally, you are expected to write a logical and balanced argument about the subject at hand.

Evaluate - This is similar to '*assess*', but here, the lecturer is asking to weigh up the performance of something which has already happened.

Explain - Here, the lecturer is asking you to relate how things work, how something happened or give reasons for certain actions.

Give an account of - Here, the lecturer is simply asking for a description.

How far...? To what extent...? - Here, the lecturer is inviting you to assess a particular situation or the truth of a statement.

Identify - Here, the lecturer is asking you to single out the main features of something.

Illustrate - Here, the lecturer is asking you to give examples, statistics, diagrams, sketches, etc. to support your statements.

Indicate - Here, the lecturer is asking you to point out the main features of something (may be employed instead of '*identify*').

Justify - Here, the lecturer is asking you to state valid evidence for accepting a particular statement or conclusion (similar to '*argue*').

List - Here, the lecturer is asking you to offer an item-by-item record of relevant items. This would normally be in note form without any need to describe - but you are best advised to ask the lecturer, if you are not sure.

Outline - Here, the lecturer is asking you to point out the main features of a particular topic or sequence of events.

Prove - Here, the lecturer is asking you to establish the truth of something by offering indisputable evidence or a logical sequence of steps or statements that establishes the truth.

Relate - Here, the lecturer is asking you (depending upon the wording of the question at hand), to give an account of how things happened or compare and contrast.

Review - Here, the lecturer is asking you to look back on, or survey, a particular topic and estimate its value (may be employed instead of '*evaluate*').

State - Here, the lecturer is asking you to write down the main points of something.

Summarise - Here, the lecturer is asking you to give the main points of an idea or argument, leaving out all the unnecessary detail.

Trace - Here, the lecturer is asking you to outline the main connections between one thing and another or to describe the development of something.

 4   ## Back to the question

Having established what '*discuss*' means, you are now in a position to relate to the question above.

The question is asking you to outline and examine the various truths and untruths in the question and having done so, offer your own opinion on whether the employment of a cultural diverse work force can truly offer the company competitive advantage over its competitors.

Now at first hand, it would appear that the simple answer to the question is 'yes'. But a closer examination tells us that employing a cultural diverse team will not, on its own, necessarily guarantee a competitive advantage for the firm concerned. You must always remember that with any assignment, the clues are always in the question and the obvious answer is not always the case.

Assuming you got this question from the lecturer, some of the tips the lecturer would probably have given - coupled with a close examination of the question - would have guided you to discuss areas pertaining to:

- Globalisation - its origins and some general background (how much detail you go into in each area will naturally depend on how many words you have to play with).

- Cultural Diversity - what is it? What are its origins? etc.

- The relation between cultural diversity and globalisation.

Note: The above structure would only really pertain to a short to medium sized essay of, say, 2000 to 4000 words. A longer essay or dissertation would necessitate the inclusion of other relevant areas and/or more detail in the existing areas.

With the above tips in mind (either obtained from the lecturer and/or derived from simply examining the question in more detail), you are now ready for the next stage, which is to obtain the necessary research for the question.

 Obtaining the research material - books or journals?

This is another key area of the assignment-writing process. After all, the quality and execution of the research material will dictate the quality of the finished product - bad tools and planning equates to a bad job.

In giving you my advice and guidance here, I would prefer to stick to my tried-and-tested method, which I have obtained in all my years of helping students write-up assignments for which they have consistently obtained excellent marks.

Further, where possible, I always try and avoid using books except where the essay requires the input of theory, which would either be outlined in the question sheet or by the lecturer in giving you tips on what to include in the assignment. The disadvantage of books is that, in the majority of cases, they only really refer to one point in time and employing their use may result in the lecturer marking you down on the accusation of "couldn't you find more recent material?".

Perhaps an example would help to illustrate this point further:

Suppose that, in relation to the essay above (cultural diversity), you were to include an area on globalisation obtained from a book (in your own words of course). Now suppose the book was last reprinted in say, 1997. There is always a risk that some of the material on globalisation may be out of date in that new theories on the subject may have been written since then. Every good essay requires the input of *recent* and *relevant* examples. The 1997 book will no doubt have examples dated around 1997, which the lecturer may deem to be too old for use in a present-day essay.

Consequently, I prefer to employ the use of journal articles. Why? Because they are up-to-date, relevant and analytical (as opposed to books, which tend to be largely descriptive) and often contain very good examples; all these factors are key ingredients of a well-written essay.

George's Tip!! — Always (i.e. current) use lots of recent examples when-ever possible when compiling your assignments

So having decided that, where does one obtain these precious journals from? Well, there are four key places which, in order of importance, are:

- Academic Institutes;

- Libraries including CD-ROM (such as FT McCarthy);

- University library;

- The Internet.

Sources and the best advice on the above are given later in this practical guide.

All the institutes will normally be in a position to provide you with a comprehensive reading list on your chosen topic. On contacting the appropriate institute, which would either be by phone or in person (depending on its proximity to your address or university), you'll be asked to provide the research assistant (at the institute) with the actual question of your assignment or give them its key words.

Now before doing so, remember that what you put in is what you get out. The computer can't read your mind so it is important that you provide the research assistant with the appropriate key words. Personally, to be on the safe side, I'd recommend that you tell him or her the actual question as well as what you consider to be the key words.

In the case of the question (on cultural diversity) above, the key words to be entered into the computer would be words like: *cultural diversity, globalisation* & *company/organisation competitive advantage*. These key words will also apply when searching on your university CD-ROM and the Internet but never forget (and I repeat): "What you put in is what you get out". Put in the wrong key words and you'll get fed the wrong articles or, perhaps even worse, articles that aren't directly relevant thus making your task harder.

Having done this, you'll be provided with a reading list of the latest journal articles say going back two to three years. Depending on the popularity of the question at hand, the researcher may only give you a reading list going back one year. If the particular topic is a popular one, it is very important that you tell the research assistant before hand how far back you want the articles to go.

Once you've received the reading list, you can either order the articles (paying by cheque or credit card) or a much cheaper method would be to obtain the articles yourselves from the library shelves.

Details of all the recommended institutes are listed in the latter part of this practical guide coupled with the tips on how to obtain the research information at minimum cost.

 ## 6 ▶ Selecting the right articles (from the reading list)

Upon receiving the reading list, one question you will probably ask yourself is "Which of the articles should I get from the reading list? Which ones are most appropriate for my essay?" At this point, perhaps it would be appropriate to give you an outline of what to expect on the reading list. The list contains various headings but the key ones you'll need to look out for are:

- Title - Title of the article;

- Serial - Serial/journal that the article comes from;

- Page number(s);

- Date - date of article (e.g. Autumn 2000; 16th of March 2001);

- Vol. - Volume of the journal (e.g. Vol.5, No.4);

- Abstract/Description - Gives you a few lines on what the article is about.

To get the articles at the cheapest price, your best bet is to attend the institute personally and photocopy the articles yourself. This could cost you as little as 10p per page (depending on where you go) compared with a cost of £4.00 per article if you choose to order through the institute. See later for more details.

Irrespective of what method you choose to obtain the articles, it will be up to you to select the articles you want to order/photocopy. Experience has taught me that the best way to choose the articles is by reading the title and abstract of the article. These two areas should give you a good indication of whether the article is relevant to your assignment question. My tip is that if you're not sure, take the article regardlessly so as to be on the safe side, especially if you're planning to visit the institute personally (which will prove to be much cheaper).

 ## 7 Making sense of the articles selected

Having selected and photocopied all the articles you want, what do you do next? Well, the next stage will be to extract the relevant pieces of information from the journals. Here, there are many possible ways but I would strongly recommend my tried-and-tested method, which I have outlined in the following.

Firstly, number all the pages of the journals from page 1, 2, 3... to the end. The reason behind this will become apparent in a minute. Secondly, get a sheet of A4-paper and on it, you'll need to write some headings that you know must feature in the essay. Every essay has compulsory headings such as *Introduction, Conclusion, Background*, etc. Likewise all essays need to have what I would term 'non-compulsory headings', which are headings that are dependent on the particular task and thus vary from assignment to assignment.

Additionally, every good essay must include areas that will maximise the student's marks by impressing the lecturer who is to mark it. These areas include theory, statistics, surveys, studies and any possible examples.

With this established, on the sheet of paper which I asked you to set aside earlier on, write down all the compulsory headings (introduction, conclusion, etc.) and areas (studies, examples, etc.) as outlined above. Having done so, your A4-sheet should now look like this:

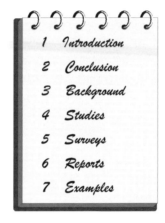

and so on.

The reason behind this is simple. What you are doing, in effect, is creating a book out of all your articles, and by listing the above, you are creating your "*Contents*" page. The benefits of this approach are numerous. For example, it allows you to know where every key area is in each article and, should you need to go back to that area, you will not have to rack your brain trying to remember where everything is. So, for example, assuming that in reading all the articles, pages 5, 9, 16, 34, 45, 47, and 55 contained relevant examples and say page 5 had an example on Texaco, 9 on British Airways, 16 on Wal Mart, 34 on British Telecom and so on, should you wish (at any point in time) to refer to that particular example, you can locate it in a matter of seconds.

George's Tip!!

Always use lots of recent (i.e. current) examples whenever possible when compiling your assignments

Having written down all the headings and areas above, and page numbered all the articles, without realising it, you would have already formed, in your mind, part of what is known as a mental picture of the essay you are about to write.

This stage is where it gets a little complicated and, as a result, you will have to concentrate fully. This is because, in reading the articles, you will in effect be writing the entire essay in your mind. Carefully read through all the articles slowly, page-by-page, line-by-line and make sure you concentrate. If possible, make sure you are in a quiet place where you can't be interrupted.

In reading through the articles, you'll need to do two important things. Firstly, remember those headings and areas written down on you sheet? Well you'd better because, in reading the articles, you will need to identify areas that match your headings as noted and areas on your A4-sheet. So, for example, in reading the first article, you'll notice that it has an introduction, a conclusion and some background. If this is the case, simply mark the relevant paragraphs in the best way you know how and scribble next to them the relevant heading (e.g. *intro*).

The article may also have an example or a study or report, which you may consider important to your assignment. If so, mark these areas as well and, as you are marking them on the article, make sure you number the relevant pages on the A4-sheet.

Secondly, there will also be areas in the article that are not on the sheet but are areas that you consider important. For example, the 'cultural diverse' article may have subheadings entitled '*What is Globalisation*'; '*The Importance of Cultural Diversity*'; '*Origins of Cultural Diversity*'; '*The Cultural Diversity Theory*' and if you're really lucky, you may hit the jackpot and find a heading or article entitled something like '*The importance of cultural diversity to organisational profits*'.

Having gone through the first one or two articles, you're A4-sheet will now begin to resemble that shown on the following page:

Interpreting this illustration tells us that pages 1, 3 & 7 of the articles, which we have read so far, have areas that can be employed as *Introductions* to our essay. Note that some of the headings haven't yet got a number. All this means is that in our reading so far, we haven't come across anything relating to those areas.

As you read on, if you see an area in any article that you feel may be relevant to the essay, simply make a note of it on the A4-sheet and in the actual article it came from.

When you have finished going through the articles, you would have built up a large contents page of relevant areas with perhaps some areas being covered a number of times. Having done this, congratulate yourself, as you've come through the hard stage. The next stage is to decide what actually goes into the essay's first draft.

> **Note: Plagiarism is a university offence, which is taken extremely seriously. There is nothing wrong with employing the use of other people's work as long as (a) you fully understand what you are reading, (b) you put their work into your own words and (c) you give them credit in your work by way of a reference or footnote. Never pass off other people's work as your own!**

Go through the contents list and, depending on the specified length of your essay, pick out the areas which you want included in the essay. At this stage, bear in mind that (a) you must include the compulsory areas and (b) this will only be the first draft. If you feel that you are not entirely happy with it, you can always chop and change until you are totally satisfied.

Having done this, pick out the first area to be included, say, the area entitled "*Cultural Diversity*" and read through all the areas bearing this tag (which you marked out earlier). Having done so and once you're sure you've fully understood them, install what you consider to be your most favourite (i.e. interesting) parts as your contribution to this area of the essay entitled "Cultural Diversity".

In doing this, try to get into your lecturer's mind and ask: "If I were the lecturer what would impress me most?" If you are able to answer this question (and there is no reason why you shouldn't be able to do so especially if you obtained the tips from him/her at the outset), you are well on your way to writing the essay.

Once you've compiled that particular section, you must then make sure that you translate it into your own words while simultaneously retaining the coherence and flow of the paragraph. You will also need to quote the reference that the section came from, which would either be at the end of the paragraph (in the article) or at the top (i.e. heading) of the article itself. This would normally be shown as a Harvard style reference (e.g. Smith, 1998) or as a footnote at the bottom of the page or in a separate "*References*" section at the end of the article.

Carry on this process throughout the essay and, before you know it, you will have finished the essay. In doing so, you would have written an essay that is:

- Relevant.
- Recent and analytical.
- Contains relevant and recent reports, studies, surveys, etc.
- Contains recent and relevant examples.
- Well-written, well-structured and flowing in an academic and professional manner.

The one thing you should note that all have in common is that they are nearly all the key items that lecturers look for in awarding you high marks.

Note: Remember the important tips which we advised you to get from your lecturer? Well, make sure you look out for them whilst reading through the research you have obtained.

8 ▶ The Introduction, Heart of the Essay and Conclusion

These three areas deserve a special mention: the first because first impressions count and the last because last impressions last whilst the heart of the essay is what the lecturer looks for to ascertain if you've understood the question properly and, in doing so, whether you've answered it correctly.

The Introduction

Here, first of all, you will need to define the topic, say what you understand by it, state the main issues and give a general idea of how you are going to deal with them.

So, for example, in the case of our Cultural Diversity question, having done the above, you will need to end the Introduction by saying something like "In attempting to ascertain/discuss whether a cultural diverse work force necessarily gives a firm competitive advantage over its rivals, perhaps it would be appropriate to begin by firstly outlining the origins of cultural diversity and globalisation."

This statement then opens the door for you to outline and discuss the surrounding areas of the assignment question prior to delving into the main body. How many words you devote to these sections will depend on how many words you have to play with in the essay. For example, assuming the essay's specified length is 3000 words, I would recommend that approximately 300 words each go to the Introduction and Conclusion, 1400 goes to the surrounding areas and the remainder - about 1200 - towards the analytical 'main body' area of the essay.

Notice that I have used the word *'attempt'*. This is the word I always feel is best to use throughout the essay as it sounds appropriate and tells the lecturer that you will do your best without sounding arrogant in that you know it all.

The Conclusion

Here you sum up your main ideas and state any firm conclusions you have come to as a result of these ideas. Say whether you consider that there are any possible wider implications, future trends or scope for further investigations. So, for example in this case, you may say "This essay has attempted to explore and discuss the notion that the employment of a cultural diverse work force gives a firm competitive advantage. In doing so, it has found that, although a cultural diverse work force can indeed give a particular company competitive advantage, various factors need to be in place for the advantage to materialise."

For example, the essay has shown that the problems of cultural clashes inherent within a cultural diverse work force need to be rectified first not to mention the fact that, if other areas of the organisation are not performing efficiently, a cultural diverse work force alone cannot, realistically, be expected to cure any ills plaguing the organisation. Future research will ideally need to explore various variables pertaining to cultural diversity and competitiveness to assess their respective compatibility.

The next stage of the conclusion can then go on to include areas found in the articles you obtained (in your own words of course). The last paragraph of the conclusion is very important as it is the last thing the lecturer will probably read prior to marking your assignment so where possible, try and add something humorous or witty without detracting from the seriousness of the essay you have just written.

If you should require the full draft of the "Cultural Diversity" essay (referred to in this section) for your own clarification, please consult the "Help and Advice" section at the rear of this guide.

The Main Body (heart of the essay)

This is where you will need to answer the question. Here you must ensure that you include any reports, surveys, studies, statistics, examples, theories, etc., that you managed to obtain through the articles you have researched. Here, you will also have to state your facts, your evidence, and illustrations and develop your argument. Note that simply stating them will not be enough. You will have to make sure that they are all in an easy-to-follow logical and consistent sequence.

So for example, you may have a paragraph that reads: "In their 1998 study, Johnson and Simpson (1998) found that, when a culturally diverse work force was employed within an organisational setting, efficiency and performance within the work force was found to increase five fold. This finding is enforced by a similar survey by Texaco in 2000 which found that within its department comprising of a cultural diverse mix, performance was noticeably higher when compared to another department within the company that primarily comprised of Caucasians."

Remember also that, at tho ond of this, the lecturer wants to see your own opinion added so as to blend in with the opinions from other sources.

All in all, don't worry if at first it all seems somewhat confusing or complicated. It took me a few months to master the art and, as you get more and more practice, you'll be pleasantly surprised by how easy it has become.

 ## 9 ▶ Looking out for the 'high mark' earners

In compiling an assignment, there are undoubtedly areas that you will have to identify so as to include them in your work. The tricky part is that is that the lecturer won't tell you what these 'golden nuggets' are. It will be up to you to find them and piece them into the assignment or dissertation.

Although these things may be small, they can make a huge difference to your work. Lecturers are impressed with small attention to detail and lots of evidence. This evidence (and the things you'll have to look out for) can come in the following forms:

- *Soundbites & Name Dropping* - opinions from experts, industry specialists and other people/organisations (such as company executives) related to your chosen subject;

- *Studies and Surveys* that may have been conducted on your chosen company and/or industry;

- *Market Reports* on your industry (from bodies such as Mintel, MAPS, etc.);

- *Company Examples* (but only recent ones) that may serve to clarify your chosen points more clearly;

- *Diagrams* including graphs, tables, charts that may serve to illustrate your points further. Incidentally, you'll need to employ the use of charts, tables and graphs to illustrate the findings of any primary research which you may carry out;

- *Theory* - You may find related theory in some of the journals but more books by well-known academics such as Michael Porter, Boston Consultancy Group (BGC Matrix), Value Chain Analysis, SWOT Analysis, PEST Analysis, etc.

  Here, perhaps we should add a note of caution: Students often feel that it is okay simply to include theory and diagrams without relating them to the subject at hand. Another big mistake. Your lecturer won't be impressed that you've gone to a book and picked out a few theories and diagrams and plumped them in the middle of your assignment. No way. However, he or she will be impressed that not only have you managed to pick out the relevant theories to employ but more importantly that you've shown your complete and utter understanding of those theories by relating them to your dissertation subject in a competent manner.

No doubt, if you've done your research correctly, you'll find rich pickings of all of the above throughout the research material. All you need to do is *(a)* pick them out, *(b)* fit them into the right area of your main body (i.e. in the right context) and *(c)* make sure you attach its source.

For example, in backing up your theory that rising costs are crippling the profits of the airline industry, you may include an example from, say, Virgin Atlantic that shows how, due to rising costs, its profits have decreased 10% over the last financial year. Such an example may have been included in a quality newspaper such as the *Financial Times*, a magazine such as *The Economist* or in an airline journal such as *The Airline Business News*.

Making recommendations

What is the best way to make suitable and feasible recommendations for your particular assignment? Simple, let the industry experts do it for you. Confused? Allow me to explain:

When collating research for any subject, making recommendations is nearly always associated with a particular company, companies, industry and/or sector. Following on from this, your required recommendations (i.e. needed by your lecturer) should propose the resolution of a particular situation besetting the particular company, industry, etc. which was embedded in the assignment question.

In collating suitable academic research for your assignment, if you have done it correctly (i.e. by the method outlined in earlier sections of this guide), you should find that you have unearthed numerous articles in quality newspapers and journals that not only discuss your chosen company and sector but, more rewardingly, make professional recommendations as to how it (i.e. the company and/or industry) can rectify the problem situation at hand. These recommendations may come in the shape of analyses carried out by industry experts and/or examples of how similar competing companies (i.e. companies within the same industry) have attempted to gain competitive advantage.

Having achieved the first stage, all you have to do then (having located these precious articles) is to understand and reword them as well as to draw on them for new ideas and inspiration and, in doing so, add your own proposals. Remember, originality always impresses the lecturer!

• Drawing on academic theory

If you are at university, the chances are that, in making your recommendations, the lecturer may expect you to draw on the use of academic theory. All this simply means is that the lecturer expects you to demonstrate your ability to employ the use of appropriate theory to illustrate your point and, in addition, to show clearly your ability to understand the theory. Simply installing a diagram or two to 'explain' what the theory is, will not do. Instead, you have to relate the theory(ies) to the case at hand.

The lecturer should be in a position to guide you on which theory(ies) to include in the assignment. Further, the best place to locate suitable theories would be in any good textbook or, if you're lucky, in certain quality academic journals. You will not find such theories in newspapers nor in market reports.

• An example

Perhaps an example may help to illustrate this point further. Let us consider conceived problems besetting British Airways. The company's passenger traffic has dropped on some routes, especially the North Atlantic routes, by as much as one-third. Now assume the question asks you to put yourself in the position of the Director of Strategy of BA and then make recommendations to the Chief Executive as to how the problems can be rectified. How do you go about it?

The first thing would be to collate suitable research that covers not only the airline itself but, more importantly, the industry as a whole and I mean the global airline industry not just the UK. During that task not only would you have found research articles that discuss the problem in detail, but you would also have found numerous

articles that analyse and evaluate BA's financial and strategic position. These articles will also discuss where BA needs to go from here (i.e. what strategy options it has to reduce the extra capacity it is suffering and thus sustain its current profitability - if not increase it).

You will also have found research that discusses what BA's direct competitors (i.e. Virgin, United Airlines, American Airlines, etc.) have done as well as its indirect competitors (e.g. Easyjet, GO, Ryanair, etc.). For example, in response to the severe downturn in traffic as a result of, say, people's reluctance to board aircraft immediately after hijackings or terrorist attacks, the competitors might (as has happened in the past) immediately reduce fares to encourage passengers to carry on boarding planes. This is known as a 'cost reduction strategy' and has proved successful with the airlines implementing the strategy all reporting higher than average figures.

Consequently, this may well be a strategy you could recommend for BA, albeit a short-term one, until passenger confidence returns. You may also want to consider other cost-cutting strategies such as using smaller, more fuel-efficient aircraft, less frequent flights, staff and wage cutting measures, etc.

The key here is that, in sifting through the research information, you should come across various ideas that other companies have used as well as ideas that the people in the know (i.e. the experts) recommend. Simply build on these ideas and, before you know it, you will find that you have a long list of feasible and impressive recommendations.

In terms of theory, the best ones that spring to mind in this case, without going into too much detail, include a SWOT and PESTAL Analysis, use of the Boston (BGC) Matrix as well as a Value Chain Analysis. You may also want to use Porter's Five Forces Theory. Again, as each case will be different, your lecturer may be the best person to advise you on the best theories to employ, although he or she is unlikely to tell you how to relate them to the given case.

> **Remember:** With any assignment, in drawing on other people's hard work, always give them recognition by way of references, put things into your own words and try to be original, as this impresses lecturers. Also, don't forget to state any reservations you may like to attach to the recommendations you have developed as well as any assumptions you have had to make.

Bibliography & References

For the references and bibliography, you'll need to include all those references that you encountered throughout the articles which you researched such as Smith, 1998; Simpson and Johnson 1998, etc. At the back of the article, you'll find the full reference of the author contained within the essay so Smith 1996 would now be listed as:

1. Smith, J. The Importance of Cultural Diversity. The General Management Journal. Vol.25 No.4 pp.39-56 February (1998).

2. Simpson, P. and Johnson, D. Globalisation and The Cultural Diverse Work Force. The Academy of Management Executive Journal. Vol.6. No.8 Fall 1998. pp.67-81

You may also choose to include other journals in your reference list that you may have read but not actually included in your essay. This is fine as you are allowed to included articles and books that you consulted although you may not necessarily have included the various author's articles in the finished essay.

Your enlarged reference list may also win you added brownie points given that lecturers are impressed with lengthy reference lists as it shows that you have done a lot of reading for his or her essay. However, make sure the reference list isn't too long as it may become unrealistic and thus unbelievable.

 ## Information overkill - what do I do?

Quite often, students find that, in reading through the research material collated, there may be areas that they feel would help the quality of their essay but including them may make the essay exceed the specified word limit. If this happens to you (and trust me, it often does) what should do you? Simple, include the information as *Appendices* and make sure you make references to it in the actual text. This is because information in the appendices does not add to the word count although it does count towards your mark. So there. I bet you didn't know that!

For example, in the main body of the essay, you may state: "There have been numerous studies conducted in the area of cultural diversity and competitive advantage that illustrate the pros and cons. Due to the word constraints associated with this essay, please refer to Appendix 2 for a small selection of these studies."

CONGRATULATIONS. YOU HAVE COMPLETED YOUR FIRST ESSAY AND, PROVIDED YOU'VE DONE IT OUR WAY, YOU'RE WELL ON YOUR WAY TO GETTING A BRILLIANT MARK!

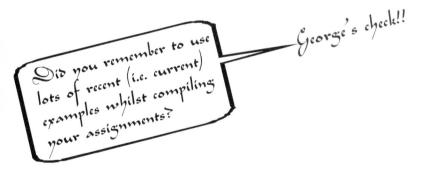

Writing Reports

Ordinarily I would not have included a section on writing reports in this guide but, from my experience of assisting hundreds of students, it would appear that report writing is becoming increasingly popular as an assessed activity. More and more assignments are requiring students to answer assignment questions in the form of reports as opposed to just straight essay formats.

 ## Who is the report addressed to?

If you're given an assignment that requires an answer in report format, what do you do? Well, as far as the basic structure goes, nothing really changes. You will still have to follow the procedures I have outlined in the preceding 'Compiling an Assignment' chapter. What will change however is the layout of the report. Remember, the report you will be required to write will have been commissioned by someone and as a result, in writing it, you will have to assume that that person will be reading it. Consequently, you will have to write it as if you were speaking to the person face-to-face.

For example, under a normal essay, a particular paragraph may read something like:

> "...given the level of impending legislation from the EC on airline safety, airlines that wish to remain competitive will need to cut costs severely and maximise efficiency."

But in a report format, remembering that the report is for the benefit of say the chief executive of a particular airline, the paragraph would need to read:

> "...given the level of impending legislation from the EC on airline safety, it is my professional opinion that, if British Airways wishes to remain competitive, it will need to cut costs severely and maximise efficiency."

The above is a very simplistic, basic example but I hope you've got the gist.

The layout and structure

The format of reports may differ slightly depending on, for example, the specific requirements of the lecturer who sets the assignment. However, given my observations in the various requests from different lecturers from universities all over the UK, the suggestion below is drawn from combining all the various styles and formats into a common layout:

- **Title page** - for example: Report into the Financial Position of British Airways

- **Terms of reference** - for example: On the request of the CEO of British Airways, to explore and analyse the long-term profitability of the airline given the advent of external forces such as EC regulations on airline safety. Sources of information were interviews, documentation, financial records, etc.

- **Contents** - Summary, Introduction to BA, Background on the Industry, etc.

- **Summary** - for example: This reports seeks to provide a detailed financial analysis, review of strategy and PESTAL analysis on BA to ascertain the long-term operation of the airline.

- **Introduction** - for example: British Airways plc is the national airline of the UK and specialises in the carriage of passengers to all continents of the world.

- **Main text** - See layout for assignments in preceding chapter.

- **Conclusions** - for example: Having analysed and evaluated all the relevant factors and conducted a PESTAL and SWOT Analysis on BA and the industry, we have come to the conclusion that...

- **Recommendations** - for example: It is recommended by ABC Management Consultants that, in order for BA to sustain its competitiveness and thus profitability into the long-term, it will need to adopt the following strategies.

- **Appendices**

Above is a general structure of a report and - in the absence of specific guidance from your lecturer - one which I would advise you follow when given a report to write.

Lastly, remember to ask yourself three important questions:

- Who is the report for?
- Has the report been written specifically for them?
- Have you backed up all your views and recommendations with evidence?

Tackling Case Studies

These days, case studies are part of the norm when it comes to students having to compile university assignments. Assignments can come in all different shapes and range from straight essays, to report compiling, making a presentation or, indeed, working on a case study.

When students hear the term 'case study' the immediate thought that enters their heads is having to read through pages-upon-pages of case material. Although this may well be the case in certain circumstances, you needn't worry because all case studies are assignments with part of the research needed to compile the assignment already provided (i.e. given to you by the lecturer as part of the assignment). This is no big deal given that, if you hadn't been given the research, you would have had to carry it out yourself anyway.

Case studies are a good method of university teaching in that they prepare students for real life scenarios that are likely to be faced in the real world post-university/college. They (case studies) usually relate to a particular company, companies, industry or sector or - in some extreme cases - all combined. The case study would typically necessitate the student having to read through the provided material and answer the problem questions at the end of the case study. Further, in most circumstances, the student is required to make recommendations as well as attempt to ascertain the reasons behind something. For example, the question can (having read through the case study material) ask the student to outline the principal factors why a particular company went into decline or why an industry or sector is having to shed jobs. In doing so, it is my guess that the case study would ask you to make feasible and logical recommendations as to how the company or industry can pick itself up.

Example Question

Perhaps a detailed example would help to make the above points clearer. Let's assume the you have been given a case study of J.Sainsbury plc which details how Sainsbury's was the leading UK grocer in the 1980s but for some reason lost its no.1 position to Tesco and as a result has been at number two since. Let us also assume that further financial evidence, as outlined in the case study, indicates that J.Sainsbury is still losing sales.

Now you (the student) are faced with the following three questions relating to the case study:

1 Having read through the case study material presented, suggest possible reasons why Sainsbury lost its position as the UK's leading grocer in the 1980s?

2 It has been suggested that Sainsbury's and other grocery retailers within its industry will perhaps find it hard to regain the level of sales once enjoyed in the late '80s to early '90s. Discuss this statement within the context of the case study.

3 Will it be possible for Sainsbury's to regain its no.1 position?

 ## Answering the questions - what is the first step?

In answering the questions, the first thing the student must always remember is that the clues are in the question. The second thing the student has to ask himself or herself is what is needed here? Is there a common threading running through all three questions? If so, what is that threading?

Now let's take all three questions. It is clear that the questions, and indeed the entire case study, centre on not only Sainsbury's but also, more importantly, the entire grocery retailing sector. Consequently, this will involve Sainsbury's competitors such as Tesco, Asda and Safeway. In short, the common threading running through the case study is Sainsbury's and the industry within which it operates.

Having ascertained this, what happens next? What happens next is that you (the student) will have to collate research (in addition to the case study material you already have) that centres on these two areas. In line with the research tips and guidelines outlined throughout this book, you will have to collate research as outlined in the following sections:

• Answering Question 1

Reworded, this question is simply asking the student to outline and discuss Sainsbury's and its problems over the years. This task is pretty straightforward in that you will have to sift through your university CD-ROM (Quality newspapers - Financial Times, The Times, Daily Telegraph, etc.), quality business and marketing journals (various academic research institutes - Institute of Management, Chartered Institute of Marketing, etc.) and market reports (Mintel, Keynotes, Market Assessment Publications or MAPs for short) for suitable research material.

If you have carried out your research correctly, you will have come across numerous articles that, in effect, answer the question for you. All you have to do is simply understand what the experts have written and translate their analyses into your own words. It is as simple as that.

Just in case you are wondering whether you might get confused over what is in the case study material and the material collated from other secondary sources, don't be. Why? Because the case study material and the material from secondary sources must be the same, after all, they are all on the same company aren't they?

However, having said that, you must always remember not to include any unnecessary material (i.e. waffle). Simply highlight the key points and list them. Your lecturer doesn't want to read irrelevant points.

Perhaps a good method would be to list the reasons as bullet points with perhaps a few lines of text to show the lecturer you haven't simply guessed the answer and that you could well have expanded on the points but didn't due to the word-count limits associated with that particular question.

Best research sources for this question?
Market reports and CD-ROM Articles

- **Answering Question 2**

With regards the second question, it becomes a little more complicated in that, this time, the lecturer wants you to not only demonstrate your knowledge of Sainsbury's but also the whole industry. So how do you go about matters this time? Well, you still employ the same research techniques as before (i.e. as above) but this time, you will also need to collate research on Sainsbury's three main competitors as well as the industry in general. In setting about answering this particular question, you will need to ask yourself (and in line with rewording the question): "Is the industry and thus the companies within it having difficulties and if so why?".

Now remember, earlier on in this section, I said that the clues are always in the question? Well, the clue here is that the question is in effect telling you that there are problems inherent within the industry but what are these problems? The question is also asking you whether these problems can be overcome? To begin answering this, you will need to collate research that principally discusses the industry over the last few years. Again, if you have done your research correctly, you will find that the same articles will not only highlight the key problems that these companies (i.e. the industry) are facing, but more importantly, whether they can be overcome and if so, how? Such articles are what I refer to as the 'golden nugget articles' in that they answer the question for you. An additional advantage here is that you will be able to draw inspiration and thus ideas from the experts and build on their analyses and suggestions.

My experience has taught me that you are likely to find the best industry research in market report research as well as quality newspapers. For example, you may find an article entitled: "Britain's ailing grocery sector. Is there a way forward for the grocery multiples?". One last tip that I find works for my students is that I always recommend, in translating the words of the experts into your own words, always try and retain their (the experts) way of writing, which is likely to impress the lecturer more as it also serves to demonstrate sophistication and intelligence.

Last but certainly not least, given this type of question, you will also need to carry out a detailed analysis on the industry sector as well as the company concerned. To do this you will require the latest market reports as well as a good textbook. In the majority of cases, you will find that the company and industry analyses necessitate the use of two types of analysis:

- A SWOT Analysis (i.e. Strengths, Weaknesses, Opportunities and Threats facing the company and industry), and

- A PESTAL Analysis (i.e. Political, Economical, Social-Cultural, Technological and Legal factors facing the company and its industry).

In doing the above, you may find for example, in certain cases, more strengths than weaknesses or plenty of economic factors and no technological factors. Should you find this to be the case, don't feel you may have carried out the analysis incorrectly, as certain companies and industries may be more susceptible to economic threats as oppose to say, technological threats. For example, the cross-channel industry may have more technological factors affecting it than political factors whereas the grocery retailing sector may have more economic factors affecting it than say technological. Each case is different.

Best research sources for this question?
Market Reports and CD-ROM Articles

Tip!!! In most marketing reports such as Mintel, towards the end of the report, you will find a section on the type of future predicted for the industry sector. You will also find other key areas such as various SWOT and PESTAL factors affecting the industry. All these listed factors can be employed in your analysis as long as you state your sources!!!

• Answering Question 3

The last question when 'translated' is asking you to make recommendations as to how - and if - Sainsbury's can regain its market share and hopefully knock Tesco off the top spot. In the Assignments section of this practical guide, you may recall that I advised you to always reword the question so as to help you to understand it better. This is because, as long as you answer the question correctly, the lecturer does not care how you go about it. Again, in collating the necessary research, you will need to look out for two categories of articles:

- Articles that go straight to the heart of the question: What can the industry as whole do to pick itself up again? and

- Articles that discuss what Sainsbury's competitors have done in their attempts to gain and sustain market share. One clear example of how Tesco toppled Sainsbury's to become the industry leader (and stay there) was its ability to be an innovator (as opposed to a follower) by being the first to introduce a Clubcard loyalty scheme. It was also the first to introduce new formats such as the Tesco Metro not to mention its highly efficient online shopping strategy.

In collating, reading and understanding the research obtained, you should be able to put yourself in the position of the Marketing Director of Sainsbury's and draw on the innovative ideas of other companies in thinking up possible new strategies for the company to adopt. Remember, you needn't confine yourself to UK grocery multiples - why not look further afield such as Europe and North America for ideas. After all, if it works there, there is no reason why it won't succeed over here!

In collating research, you will also find suggestions made by industry analysts and experts as to how Sainsbury's can pick itself up again. Such articles will also outline any reservations that the experts may have. For example, an industry expert may (in analysing and evaluating Sainsbury's present position) recommend the company seeks a merger or takeover of a competitor but may also highlight the fact that the company's cash flow may be severely dented in the process and consequently, may not sustain the company through the troubled times ahead should it proceed with what could well be a dangerous strategy in the short-term but potentially rewarding one in the long-term. In short, the lecturer wants you (the student) to think and write as an industry expert and, in doing so, put both sides of the argument forward. This is why at times, you will get assignment questions that, at the end, ask you to state any limitations, reservations and assumptions you may have.

> Best research sources for this question?
> Market Reports, CD-ROM Articles and Academic Journals

 ### Drawing on academic theory

If you are at university, the chances are that, in making your recommendations, the lecturer may expect you to draw on the use of academic theory. All this simply means is that the lecturer looks to you to demonstrate your ability to employ the use of appropriate theory so as to illustrate your point and also to demonstrate clearly your ability to understand the theory. Simply installing a diagram or two and explaining what the theory is will not do. Instead, you have to relate the theory(ies) to the case at hand.

Most definitely, such a question will need you to employ the use of various theories relating to the subject. The lecturer should be in a position to guide you on what theory(ies) to include in the assignment although, in this particular case, theories such as Porter's Five Forces springs to mind amongst others.

Further, the best place to locate suitable theories would be in any good textbook or, if you are lucky, in certain quality academic journals. You will not, however, find them in newspapers or market reports.

Although the above detailed example has centred on one company
and industry, it can be applied to any company and/or industry. The
idea is that, if you can understand and master the technique, you can
apply it to any case study scenario and hopefully get top marks in the
process. If the case study was on British Airways, you can draw on
strategies employed by Virgin Atlantic, Singapore Airlines, American
Airlines, etc. for ideas and inspiration. If it was on British Telecom,
you could draw on AT&T of the US and Telewest while, if it was on
Marks and Spencer's, you could draw on the winning strategies
employed by competitors like GAP and Next for ideas and inspiration.
The whole gist here is that once you have grasped the technique, you
can tackle any case study (or assignment for that matter) on any
company and/or industry - in any subject. Tackling a case study
needn't be harrowing ever again. Instead, it will be a breeze.

Remember: The wording of the case study question(s) may not
always state the obvious. No, that would be too easy! Instead, the
lecturer may want you to find that out for yourself so always examine
the question(s) very closely. With case studies, you will find that a
diagnosis of the particular company's/industry's problems, plus
suitable and feasible recommendations to rectify those problems, are
nearly always required although this may not be clearly stated in the
question. So be vigilant - the clues are always in the question!!!

On the following page is a summary of the main points which I have
made in this section on Case Studies; upon being given any case
study, simply follow the steps in the table:

4 **To summarise:**

Reword the question(s) to suit yourself and not the lecturer. Understanding the question is usually the key to correctly answering any assignment question and getting maximum marks;

Put yourself in the lecturer's shoes. What are the key things he or she is looking for in this case study assignment? Have you asked him or her for any tips on what key things they want to see in it? (refer to the earlier section in this practical guide entitled: Assignments - Receiving the assignment in a lecture or tutorial;

Find the common threading that runs through all the questions;

Ascertain the key areas - i.e. what company(ies), industry, sector, etc;

Collate the necessary research whilst simultaneously looking for the 'high earning' articles (i.e. golden nuggets);

Remember to use market reports, statistics, studies, surveys, soundbites, etc. where relevant;

When making recommendations, draw on the ideas of your company's competitors as well as the industry experts. With the latter, try and match their style of writing whilst remembering not to copy their words;

Draw on suitable academic theory where possible and relate them to the case in question. Simply mentioning them will not do;

Make sure you give credit where credit is due and always list your references as omitting these may lose you valuable marks!!

Should you need any additional advice on this section or on any area within this guide, simply refer to the help and advice page at the back of this guide.

Dissertations

Picking your Project Supervisor

In setting about writing your dissertation, you will be required to select a Project Supervisor who will not only guide you in writing your dissertation but, fortunately for you (or unfortunately depending on who you pick), will also be the main marker of your finished project. In short, they're going to be God for the duration of your project and through the marking sequence.

So how do you set about picking the right lecturer to supervise your project? My experiences, in speaking to hundreds of different students as well as guiding them, has taught me that the ideal profile of your intended Project Supervisor will need to be someone who is laid back, not too picky or fussy, a generous marker and someone who is always willing and able to help. However, having said that, this may act as a disadvantage as the 'chosen one' may expect more from your dissertation given all the time and effort they have dedicated to you.

The type of supervisor you don't want is someone who is a perfectionist, a trainee who may have just finished his or her PhD or Masters and is out to prove a point to the university hierarchy. Neither do you want a supervisor who is stingy on marks or who is always smiling - life has taught me never to trust anyone who smiles too much!

Another mistake that students tend to make is that they feel it appropriate to pick someone who they perceive as their friend. Whatever you do, make sure you do not pick a lecturer as your supervisor because you feel he or she is your friend. Why? Because firstly, no lecturer is your friend when it comes to marking your dissertation (remember that the dissertation will have a second marker so he or she will need to be honest, if they want to keep their jobs) and secondly, because your 'so-called' friend may come to expect more from you in terms of the quality of your work and, again, this will be reflected in the marking.

Instead, I would strongly advise that you choose perhaps one of your lecturers who has not only marked your work in the past but also someone who has awarded you (on average) high marks. This is simply because, for one, this would seem to indicate that they like your style of writing and, as a result, why should that suddenly change when it comes to your dissertation? My guess is that it won't.

 ## 2 A win-win situation - become the teacher's pet

Okay, I know that at this stage you're probably saying to yourself "No way am I going to lick the boots of my project supervisor!". My response to you is that this is not the time to be hard or let your pride, ego and reputation get in the way. After all, who will know apart from you and your supervisor?

From the moment you get assigned or pick your supervisor, make sure you compliment and flatter them as and when appropriate but don't overdo it. Let them know that you value their opinion and be sure to occasionally defer to them with comments such as: "Well sir/ma'am, given that you are an expert on this matter, I felt it appropriate to consult you first before..." or perhaps: "Given your vast experience and knowledge in this area, could you give me advice on whether adopting this approach (or including this area) would be of relevance?".

Doing the above will serve to benefit you in many ways, including:

- Showing your supervisor that you value his or her opinion;

- Showing your supervisor that you've consulted them all the way through your writing the project and, in the process, gained from their 'expert' advice and judgment. To fail you or give you a low mark would in effect mean them giving themselves a low mark. After all, he or she co-wrote it with you, didn't they?

- Even if they didn't really give you detailed advice (some lecturers can be coy or elusive when it comes to supervising your dissertation), the fact that you've consulted them regularly (or at least attempted to consult them) shows your seriousness and dedication even if the finished article is not up to expectations. No lecturer will fail you having seen that you at least made a concerted effort.

And last but certainly not least, be sure to include them in your acknowledgments by stating something like:

"And I would like to give a special mention and express my gratitude to my Project Supervisor Dr..., Mr..., Ms... for his/her unequivocal support, patience and guidance during the writing of this dissertation."

Now tell me, what lecturer will mark you down after reading such a tribute?

 ## 3 Choosing the dissertation subject

Let's go back a step. Imagine that it is close to the end of the last term just before the long Summer break and you've been informed by your tutor that, for your final year, you're going to have to hand in a dissertation, which (according to most universities) will count as two modules towards your final mark in year 3 (your final year).

The majority of universities let you go away on vacation to decide on a subject proposal to be submitted early in the final year (around October/November). The universities give you all this time for a perfectly good reason. Because, once you pick a subject for your dissertation and it has been approved by your supervisor, you won't be allowed to change midway; hence the reason why you are given ample time to consider and make the decision.

So what do you do? For a start, one thing you don't do is pick a topic off the top of your head and neither do you choose a topic simply because it happens to be dear to your heart, is your hobby, your country of origin, etc. By all means, select a subject about which you feel adequately knowledgeable. However, the contributory factors that go towards your decision must stretch much further than "Well, I chose it because it's my hobby." or "This particular topic was the first thing that came into my head."

In my years of guiding students on writing their final year dissertations, I often found that students tend to overlook this area as if it weren't an important part of the dissertation process. Big mistake. For example, I once got a student who wanted to write about "The tourism industry in Greece" and another who wanted to write about "The IT industry in India". On first sight, both choices would appear to be quite interesting topics to write about for final year academic dissertations. However, when I asked both students how they planned on getting enough quality academic research material to sustain these dissertations from beginning to end, one response was "I was hoping that there will be adequate material in my library" whilst the other stated "I hadn't put much thought to it up till now. It just sounded like a good idea at the time."

I advised them that, based on my extensive knowledge in carrying out academic research, they would be hard pushed to find quality academic research material in any UK library (university or public) and neither would they find any decent information in any academic research institute. Now, no-one is saying that there isn't any information on these two topics in libraries or book shops but one question you have to ask yourself is whether there is *enough* quality research material to sustain the specified length of the dissertation (normally 10,000 words)? I think not and the students appeared to agree by their respective decisions to opt for subjects recommended by myself.

The important point being made here is that the choice of your dissertation topic must be taken with caution and care. It should be the most important decision you make in going about writing your dissertation. It's no use picking a subject only to find, halfway, that you haven't got enough quality research material to finish off the job. If you think that you can just simply go to your lecturer with your problem, think again, as his/her response is likely to be "that's not my problem. You were given plenty of time to think about a topic and I'm afraid that the university regulations don't permit me to allow you to change subjects at this late stage. You're just going to have to stick with it."

Remember that, in the final analysis, your supervisor doesn't care what topic you pick for your dissertation. All they care about is that it is well-researched and well written. Likewise, in choosing a topic, you have to ask yourself the all-important question which is "What matters to me more: a high mark with a popular topic, where there's probably lots of good quality research material, or a remote yet interesting topic, where there's very little (if any) research material?"

If you picked the former, then you're well on your way to obtaining a high mark for your dissertation and, hopefully, degree. The beauty of dissertations, as opposed to the majority of assignments, is that you have total control over the content of your dissertation. Consequently, the question isn't whether you pass or fail it (as it's impossible to fail) but more, how high a mark you get for it. By using this guide properly, we'll make sure you get that all-important high mark.

 Choosing the dissertation topic

Any financial advisor will tell you that the size of your gross annual income dictates the size of your mortgage offer. Likewise, the availability of good quality academic research should be the sole basis of your decision on what subject you should adopt for your dissertation. It is vital that you thoroughly research your chosen topic prior to submitting it as part of your proposal.

My advice would be to pick three subjects of your choice and make preliminary research enquiries as to the availability of quality academic research on all of them. Having done this, you'll be in a position to decide which to choose. This process may take a considerable amount of time but, trust me, you'll be thankful you did it in the end.

Getting the subject title approved -
(don't allow yourself to be led by your Project Supervisor)

On first appearances, this advice may seem like we are advocating that you rebel against your Project Supervisor. Don't worry, we wouldn't advocate any such thing. What this stage means is basically this: After carrying out the stages above and deciding on a dissertation title/area, then upon presenting it to your supervisor, whatever you do, do not allow yourself to be coerced into writing about a topic that is dear to your supervisor's heart (i.e. his or her choice). Supervisors have a habit of getting students to write-up projects on subjects that they want to learn more about themselves but haven't got the time to research.

What often ends up happening is that the student, in their attempt to please the supervisor, starts a project only to come unstuck halfway through. Try going to your supervisor then and telling him or her that you are having problems. What you may get is a sympathetic ear but one thing you won't hear is "No problem. Why don't you go and pick a different subject?". You are more likely to get: "I merely gave you my advice. It was up to you to fully research the topic prior to deciding on it as your dissertation title." as a response.

The point being made here is that once you have painstakingly, albeit provisionally, researched your chosen topic, stick with it and don't let your Project Supervisor talk you out of it (unless, of course, they have a very good reason why you should change subjects). Further, if having been given the OK by your supervisor, you wish to make changes, do not feel scared to ask him or her for permission. You'll find that supervisors are pretty reasonable and flexible as long as you can justify your actions.

Allow me to give you an example to clarify this. A while ago, a student came to us and decided to do a dissertation on the world's airlines. He wanted to examine the world's top five airlines (by amount of passengers carried) and examine (by way of ratio analysis) which of the five was the most profitable. Unfortunately for him, two of the five airlines were American based (United Airlines and American Airlines) while one was based in Singapore (Singapore Airlines). Upon starting the dissertation, the student found that although he could obtain the last year's annual accounts for all the airlines, when it came to obtaining accounts for the last five years (which is what would have been needed to conduct a thorough and comprehensive evaluation and analysis), only the accounts for two of the airlines (British Airways and KLM) were easily available. UA and AA said that they could only provide accounts going back one year and Singapore Airlines didn't even have any accounts to supply.

Consequently, we advised the student to go back to his Project Supervisor and request that he be allowed to alter the subject from analysing five airlines (for which he couldn't obtain sufficient accounts to sustain a detailed and comprehensive analysis) to analysing just one airline (BA). After explaining his problem, the supervisor agreed and, with our assistance, the student ended-up getting a first class mark (89%) for the dissertation.

Again, the important point being made here is that what matters, at the end of the day, is that you (as the student) get a high mark. What doesn't really matter is the choice of subject. It is better to pick a popular company or industry where there is much quality research material than an obscure company or industry where there is very little research written on it. Should you have any further difficulties in this department, you may wish to consult our academic advice and support hotline. You'll find contact details at the back of this guide.

 6 Compiling the project proposal

Having reached this stage and as long as you have followed the advice laid out in this practical guide and, in the process, worked closely with your Project Supervisor, there should be no anxiety or worry on your part on what might go wrong.

As you work on your proposal, it is imperative that you bear in mind its importance. In effect, it is an implicit contract between you and your

Project Supervisor and thus the university. You are expected to carry out the proposal to the letter, unless the supervisor (as outlined above) approves any subsequent changes you request.

You will find that universities vary in their proposal requirements so it is advisable, prior to setting out your dissertation proposal, that you consult your university handbook which specifies the procedures for writing and submitting dissertations. However, what is not ambiguous are the components of the proposals.

All proposals include three major components which are:

- Introduction to the study (aim, objectives, background to the study).

- Literature Review.

- Methodology.

• **Aim of the dissertation**

The proposal needs to begin with a couple of paragraphs that serve to introduce the reader into the dissertation. Experience has taught me that the simplest way to accomplish this goal is to state the purpose or aim of the proposed dissertation. Here is an example: "This dissertation attempts to employ the use of ratio analysis to examine the profitability and efficiency of British Airways over the last five financial years. This first chapter of the proposal introduces the dissertation."

• **Background of the dissertation**

The background usually serves to present the reader with the context to your dissertation. It may explain the external factors that might have a significant influence over the dissertation. In the case of the above example, it may introduce the reader to the background of the world airline industry and the problem befalling British Airways.

This may be stated in the following way:

"According to a recent study conducted by D'Angelo (2000), the world airline industry is set for a downturn in passenger numbers. This problem is most acute on North Atlantic routes where competition is set to be cut-throat. Consequently, the airlines that survive are those that either decrease costs and increase efficiency by pursuing whatever strategies they deem appropriate. In light of this evidence, this dissertation sets out (or attempts) to critically evaluate and analyse the efficiency and profitability of British Airways over the last five financial years. In short, the dissertation asks:

How high is British Airways flying in terms of profitability?"

A couple of times in the above quotations (and below), I have used the word '*attempt*'. This is intentional and very important as it tells the reader that "I endeavour to..." as opposed to "I will...". Ensure that you always use the word '*attempt*' as, although it is only one small word, it can make a huge difference. Trust me.

- **Objectives of the dissertation**

The objective of the dissertation is usually simply a follow-on from the aim of the dissertation. It merely breaks down the aim into smaller pieces. So, in following-on from the example above, the objectives may be to attempt to:

» Examine the background to the World Airline industry.

» Obtain and analyse the financial accounts of BA over the last five financial years.

» Outline and evaluate the strategies the airline has employed over the same period.

» Employ the use of primary research by way of an interview and/or questionnaires to support my analysis.

» Make feasible and logical recommendations as to how the airline can sustain and/or improve its financial (and non-financial) position in the long-term.

So as you can see, although I have outlined five objectives for the dissertation above, they all, in effect, culminate in the same aim, which is to attempt to examine the profitability and efficiency of BA over the last five years. I'm quite sure that you'll agree that, in order to successfully execute the aim, a great deal of research will be required into all five objectives outlined above.

- **Hypotheses**

Some dissertation requirements may require that you write up what is referred to as a 'problem statement'. Many problem statements include hypotheses, which is the researcher's (i.e. yourself) prediction or expectation of what the results will show.

There are two basic types of hypothesis: a research hypothesis and a null hypothesis.

Research Hypothesis

A research hypothesis is used when the hypothesis is stated in positive form. An example of research hypothesis, in line with the example employed above, would be as follows: "There is a positive relationship between an airline's use of smaller more economical aircraft such as the new Boeing 777 (as opposed to larger aircraft such as the Boeing 747-400) and its level of relative efficiency and profitability."

Null Hypothesis

On the other hand, in experimental and quasi-experimental studies, the problem is often framed as a null hypothesis. A null hypothesis is a negative form of the hypothesis; it is a statement that the differences have occurred because of a chance. The research study will attempt to determine if the null hypothesis is rejected or accepted.

Again, consistent with the example employed throughout this area of compiling dissertations, an example of a null hypothesis might be: "There would appear to be a correlation between the use of smaller and newer aircraft in the carriage of passengers across long distances and an airline's efficiency and profitability." Consequently, the dissertation or research study may seek to disprove or approve of such a hypothesis.

- **Rationale for focussing on the subject of...**

Although no books, practical guides nor university guidelines tell you this, my experience with students and the resultant marks for their dissertations (as well as guiding students throughout their dissertation, we always requested feedback from them in order to ascertain what fruits resulted from our joint effort) has shown that supervisors always welcome an insert in the proposal which informed the lecturer of the student's principal reasons for picking this particular topic as a subject for their dissertation. Students have picked such topics because "It is an area which I would like to explore in more detail when I graduate" or "I intend to seek a job in this company when I graduate so what better way to impress and learn about the company than by basing my entire dissertation on it."

- **The Literature Review**

Your proposal will need to include a review of the theoretical literature. The theoretical review should provide a basis for the empirical review that usually follows. The best way to accomplish this goal is by reviewing the theories typically employed in studying the problem you have identified or by developing a conceptual framework.

One quick and easy way to compile a literature review is via the aid of academic journals. The first step would be to gather academic journals and books in your chosen area. In the case of our example above, journals and books would need to concentrate firstly on the world airline industry, secondly on British Airways and thirdly on any other airline (as there is bound to be some quality background and related information on our chosen subject here).

The next step is quite simple. In reading through the material (which you'll need to do anyway as I will outline and discuss below), you will have to pick out and highlight various pieces of theory that relate to your chosen topic. For example: certain sections in the journals and books may contain phrases like "According to Johnson and Walker (1999), the world airline industry is..."; "The airlines that will emerge unscathed through the current recession are the airlines that readjust their costs and marketing strategies. This is because.... (Ajuga and Murray, 2001)." The trick will be to locate such phrases and include them as part of your literature review but remember; simply just inserting them in your dissertation won't be enough. You're going to have to make sure they're relevant as well as ensure that they are inserted and flow in a coherent manner.

> **Note: Be sure to include the full reference for any work you've employed in your literature review in your dissertation. You'll find this at the back of the article from where you obtained the reference.**

But what if it isn't so easy? What if the entire article or book makes no reference to other authors? Should this be the case, don't despair. The task is made slightly harder but not impossible. You'll just have to look harder that's all and the reference will obviously be the author of the article (found at the beginning of the particular article - in the case of a journal/serial - or in front of the book).

- **Methodology**

The methodology (sometimes referred to as the research methodology), as the name suggests, outlines the strategies (methods) you're going to adopt so as to execute successfully the aim and objectives (and if applicable hypothesis) of the dissertation. It has two principal advantages which are that it enables you to systemise your decisions about the methods you plan to use, and it enables your Project Supervisor to ensure that the methodology you plan to adopt is sound.

There are any number of ways that a methodology can follow but a general pattern that will apply to the majority of dissertations will include:

- » Type of research (primary and secondary)
- » Context and access
- » Participants and how selected
- » Instrumentation
- » Data collection
- » Data analysis

There may not be a need to include all of the above in your methodology and a more simplistic method would be to have two headings entitled 'primary research' and 'secondary research'.

Primary research refers to research obtained first hand. This can be by way of interviews, questionnaires, etc. Secondary research refers to research obtained second-hand (i.e. from books, journals, newspapers, serials, market reports, etc.). In this case you are relying on other people's research and, as a result, they need to be credited accordingly.

Having outlined how you propose to carry out your primary research, your supervisor will also want to know any limitations and problems you foresee (if you are about to conduct it) and experienced (having conducted it). To what extent did your perceived limitations materialise? Was the research easier or harder than you envisaged? With hindsight, how would you go about changing things assuming you could do things all over again?

Although the majority of books, practical guides and university guidelines don't include this process, for relatively little effort it is a huge mark gainer as the outcome really impresses supervisors, showing him or her that not only have you gone out of your way to obtain primary research but also that you fully understand what you're doing.

Conducting primary research for your dissertation is detailed in a later section of this practical guide.

Secondary research merely lists the various source headings from which you expect to obtain your research material. A typical pattern may be as follows:

> **CD-ROM: Financial Times, The Independent, The Economist, etc.**
> **Institute of Management - Journals, Serials, magazines, etc.**
> **University and Public Library - Books, Magazines & Market Reports**
> **TV - Panorama, The Money Programme, etc.**

 ## Carrying out primary research

Having decided on the area, written the proposal and had it accepted and approved by your lecturer, the next stage will be to carry out your primary research strategy. Now this stage will have to be thought out very carefully as you are now relying on someone else (who is probably a very busy person) to assist you with research material.

In my experience, I have often found that students tend to write to the head of a department (of a particular company) such as the Marketing Manager, Head of Personnel, the Managing Director, etc. This is the wrong approach to take. Firstly, because they are probably much too busy to reply to such individual requests. Secondly, because the chances are that they probably receive hundreds of requests at that particular time of year for information like yours (especially if it is a big company) - so what makes you so special. Thirdly, because, in not putting a name on the request envelope, the chances are that your letter and thus its contents will not be taken seriously. Instead, what you're likely to get is a standard and polite letter declining an interview or request for specific information.

Instead, what we advise students to do is firstly make a preliminary phone call to a company on your list and obtain the name of the head and assistant head of your chosen department. Whilst you are in contact it would be beneficial to ascertain that company's policy on providing students, like yourself, with interviews and/or specific information.

For example, companies like British Airways tend to decline specific requests for information and interviews, which is understandable given that they are a big company which probably gets hundreds (if not thousands) of requests each year. Instead, they provide students with a standard 'student pack' of information as well as directing students to the company website.

Companies cannot cope with all the requests for information and so tend to 'fob off' enquirers with such things as 'information packs' - usually good PR for the company but of little or no use at all to you if you're looking to concentrate on a specific part of the organisation.

Asking for the impossible

Some students tend to ask for the impossible and are, in effect, wasting their time. For example, students may write off to a company naively asking for information of their marketing and promotional strategies over the last couple of years and, if possible, the future or even a particular company's recruitment strategy - no chance!

Ask yourself this question. If you were the Head of Marketing of a company, would you release such important and confidential information to someone 'claiming to be a student'? For all the company knows, the caller could be a competitor masquerading as a student.

What to do

Remember that, although your dissertation would do well to have primary research contained within it, it will also do well to have evidence of a serious attempt to obtain such primary research. In other words, if you've written off to a company or several companies within the same industry and you got back rejection letters, this still counts as primary research albeit an unsuccessful attempt.

Consequently, I would suggest that, even if your chosen company is a well-known company with very little chance of giving you the research material that you want, you should still write as you will need the response letters (on headed company paper) to show as evidence in your appendices.

Your supervisor will not reduce your marks for want of trying. In fact, one could go as far to argue that it is more beneficial to you if you get declined as you can rely solely on secondary research material while simultaneously gaining marks for primary research (not carried out but still gaining recognition).

The 'cowboy' way of obtaining primary research:

When compiling primary research, in the past, certain students (short of time) have been known to go about obtaining and analysing primary research in what can best be described as 'unorthodox' ways.

In the case of an interview, for example, what they did was to fabricate a genuine letter from their chosen company and alter the words to suit their requirements. By such manipulation, a letter of rejection from British Airways could be amended to an 'accept' letter or, better still, amended to include 'answers' to questions put to the person the letter is addressed to.

Another method often adopted by students was to construct their own questionnaires and answer them themselves in a manner that points towards (and thus reinforces) the theory that the student wishes to prove in his or her dissertation. So, for example, assuming that you were looking to prove that a decline in airline prices induces people to travel more, a questionnaire designed for such a purpose can be answered in such a way that it would appear that the majority of the 'hypothetical' respondents agreed with the hypothesis. How will your supervisor ever find out?

Whereas the chances of being detected by the above methods are very slim, any student choosing to adopt these approaches does so at his or her peril. You have been warned!

This practical guide does not delve into detail on how to write interview request letters, construct questionnaires or analyse your findings, as there are a great number of books that guide you on doing this.

8   Structuring and going on to write the dissertation

The beauty of dissertations is that, ultimately, you decide what goes in them and, as a result, it is impossible to fail. Any student that fails their dissertation, due to matters relating to the content of their dissertation, deserves to be put in front of a firing squad and shot!

Dissertations are constructed in a manner that make them fail-proof. The reasons why universities do not dictate the content (only in some cases the layout and format) is so that the student is completely free to include, as content, what he or she chooses. All the university asks is that the content is directly related to your degree. So, if for example, you were studying hospitality and tourism, writing a dissertation on the Death Penalty in Texas, USA, would be inadvisable.

Another ill-advised approach and one that I found students often make is that they decide on the contents of the dissertation prior to deciding on what research material to use. In other words, they list their contents page then set about trying to locate the research to match that content. Wrong move! You can't put the cart before the horse.

If you have been given the freedom to decide on what goes into your dissertation in terms of content, why waste the opportunity and, in the process, make life harder for yourself? Surely the better option (and one which I would strongly recommend) would be to get the research first and then, having read through it thoroughly, decide on your content? At least that way, you don't come unstuck half way through writing the dissertation by way of either not having enough quality research material to sustain the dissertation all the way through or running out of research half way through.

George's Tip!!

Always use lots of recent (i.e. current) examples whenever possible when compiling your dissertation.

By sticking to my tried-and-tested method, you should end up with a dissertation that is full of quality academic content plus you don't have that added worry of wondering whether you will have enough research material for the 10,000 or so words that you have to write.

A Hollywood film producer doesn't get the cast, film crew and storyline together before first making sure that the budget to make the film is available. So why compile the contents page and do the proposal for your Project Supervisor prior to obtaining the most important thing of all for the project - the research material?

 ## 9 ▶ Obtaining the research material

The same process for obtaining research material for your dissertation is exactly the same process you would employ for researching your assignment and one, which I have fully outlined in earlier sections of the guide. The only difference here is that you'll be doing it on a much bigger scale. Consequently, I recommend you follow exactly the same process but with greater diligence.

 ## 10 ▶ Utilising the research

Having obtained and assembled all the research articles which you feel you may need for the dissertation (remembering that it is always wise to obtain much more information than you think you'll need), the next stage will be to convert the research material into your dissertation and into your own words.

Even though I stated above that it is not advisable to decide on the contents of the dissertation prior to assembling and meticulously reading through the research material, there are however, certain areas of the content, which must be included in the dissertation.

Those areas are as follows:

- Introduction
- Background (on your chosen company and/or industry)
- Literature Review
- Recommendations
- Conclusions

With the above, what I would call 'compulsory content' in mind, when reading through the research material you've assembled, you will need to select areas of the research which you consider may be ideal for your introduction, background, recommendations, conclusions, etc. What you are doing here is drawing on the ideas of the experts and, having understood and translated their work into your own words, it should also serve to inspire you to come up with your own ideas and to add to it. In other words, what you are doing is drawing on other people's academic endeavours and building upon it - something authors do all the time.

In the majority of journal and other articles, you will find that they all have abstracts, introductions, backgrounds, (perhaps) a literature review, recommendations (depending on the type of article) and always a conclusion. There is nothing wrong with drawing on these great pieces of work and converting to your own words (with references to credit the original authors for their respective contributions).

The Main Body

Having compiled all the compulsory areas of your paper, the next stage will be to assemble the content for your main body. This is something you will need to do after having read through the research material assembled. Why? Because in reading through all these articles, you're bound to come across sections of the journals that will add rich and quality academic content to your dissertation - after all, you want good marks don't you? It's akin to a writer going from restaurant-to-restaurant or city-to-city looking for inspiration for his or her next novel or a landscape painter travelling the length and breadth of the countryside looking for inspiration for his next painting or indeed an Internet entrepreneur travelling to different countries looking for ideas to emulate in his or her home country. See what you're doing (in reading through the research material) as drawing inspiration for the great dissertation you are about to write.

Still confused? Perhaps a brief example may help to clarify things better. The example employed throughout this section is that we are writing about British Airways and, in the process, the world airline industry. In doing so, and having assembled all the research material needed, let's say that a particular journal has a section on impending legislation on aircraft safety that the experts forecast will add to the operational running costs of airlines.

Further, assume another article writes in detail about the inverse relation between costs and profits in the airline industry and, in doing so, contains a brief interview with an airline executive. What you will need to do is include these two interesting areas in your dissertation 'main body' content as you don't need to be Einstein to know that they will make for interesting reading for (and hopefully impress) your project supervisor.

Naturally, you will have to read through the articles thoroughly and put them into your own words while simultaneously making sure that they flow in a coherent and consistent manner. For example, an area of the finished article (having read through a few journals) in your dissertation may be transcribed to read:

"According to a study conducted by *The Academy for Airline Safety* in 1999, leading airlines are having to face up to spiralling costs in their need to address the increasing concerns of airline passengers. This has been partly brought on by the recent spate of airline accidents of which there were four in the last year alone (Flight International 1998). Further, this is compounded with impending legislation by the European Commission (EC) in conjunction with the Civil Aviation Authority (CAA) (Airline Business News; 2000)."

" This spells bad news for the world's airlines especially given that the 'open skies' agreement has resulted in cut-throat price wars between airlines to leading European and North American destinations. These fears are echoed by Bob Eddington, Chief Executive of British Airways, who recently stated that "this is extremely worrying for leading airlines like British Airways, which is why the Government has to relax its mergers and competition policy to allow us to form a coalition with American Airlines."

"This way, we won't be forced to pass on our added costs to passengers, who will be the ultimate bearers of any added costs forced upon us as a result of this upcoming and - might I add - unwarranted legislation." (Smith, 2000, in The Financial Times)."

12 ▶ Looking out for the Golden Nuggets (i.e. brownie points)

In writing any piece of academic work, be it a 1,000-word essay or a 15,000-word dissertation, there are undoubtedly 'golden nugget' areas that you will have to look out for so as to include them in your work. The tricky part is that the lecturer won't tell you what these golden nuggets are. It will be up to you to find them and piece them into the assignment or dissertation.

Although these things may be small, they can make a huge difference to your work. Lecturers are impressed with small attention to detail and lots of evidence. This evidence (and the things you'll have to look out for) can come in the following forms:

- *Soundbites & Name Dropping* - opinions from experts, industry specialists and other people/organisations (such as company executives) related to your chosen subject;

- *Studies and Surveys* that may have been conducted on your chosen company and/or industry;

- *Market Reports* on your industry (from bodies such as Mintel, MAPS, etc.);

- *Company Examples* (but only recent ones) that may serve to clarify your chosen points more clearly;

- *Diagrams* including graphs, tables, charts that may serve to illustrate your points further. Incidentally, you'll need to employ the use of charts, tables and graphs to illustrate the findings of any primary research which you may carry out;

- *Theory* - You may find related theory in some of the journals but more books by well-known academics such as Michael Porter, Boston Consultancy Group (BGC Matrix), Value Chain Analysis, SWOT Analysis, PEST Analysis, etc.

  Here, perhaps we should add a note of caution: Students often feel that it is okay simply to include theory and diagrams without relating them to the subject at hand. Another big mistake. Your lecturer won't be impressed that you've gone to a book and picked out a few theories and diagrams and plumped them in the middle of your assignment. No way. However, he or she will be impressed that not only have you managed to pick out the relevant theories to employ but more importantly that you've shown your complete and utter understanding of those theories by relating them to your dissertation subject in a competent manner.

No doubt, if you've done your research correctly, you'll find rich pickings of all of the above throughout the research material. All you need to do is *(a)* pick them out, *(b)* fit them into the right area of your main body (i.e. in the right context) and *(c)* make sure you attach its source.

For example, in backing up your theory that rising costs are crippling the profits of the airline industry, you may include an example from, say, Virgin Atlantic that shows how, due to rising costs, its profits have decreased 10% over the last financial year. Such an example may have been included in a quality newspaper such as the *Financial Times,* a magazine such as *The Economist* or in an airline journal such as *The Airline Business News.*

13 ▶ Making Recommendations

What is the best way to make suitable and feasible recommendations for your dissertation? Simple, let the industry experts do it for you. Confused? Allow me to explain:

Recommendations are usually a must for any serious dissertation irrespective of word length or area. Although dissertations by their very nature do not necessitate the lecturer setting you a particular problem question, in submitting your dissertation draft you will normally be expected to make recommendations of some kind.

When collating research for any subject, making recommendations is nearly always associated with a particular company, companies, industry and/or sector. Following on from this, your required recommendations (i.e. needed by your lecturer) should propose the resolution of a particular situation besetting the particular company, industry, etc. which was embedded in the assignment question.

In collating suitable academic research for your assignment, if you have done it correctly (i.e. by the method outlined in earlier sections of this guide), you should find that you have unearthed numerous articles in quality newspapers and journals that not only discuss your chosen company and sector but, more rewardingly, make professional recommendations as to how it (i.e. the company and/or industry) can rectify the problem situation at hand. These recommendations may come in the shape of analyses carried out by industry experts and/or examples of how similar competing companies (i.e. companies within the same industry) have attempted to gain competitive advantage.

Having achieved the first stage, all you have to do then (having located these precious articles) is to understand and reword them as well as to draw on them for new ideas and inspiration and, in doing so, add your own proposals. Remember, originality always impresses the lecturer!

• Drawing on academic theory

If you are at university, the chances are that, in making your recommendations, the lecturer may expect you to draw on the use of academic theory. All this simply means is that the lecturer expects you to demonstrate your ability to employ the use of appropriate theory to illustrate your point and, in addition, to show clearly your ability to understand the theory. Simply installing a diagram or two to 'explain' what the theory is, will not do. Instead, you have to relate the theory(ies) to the case at hand.

The lecturer should be in a position to guide you on which theory(ies) to include in the assignment. Further, the best place to locate suitable theories would be in any good textbook or, if you're lucky, in certain quality academic journals. You will not find such theories in newspapers nor in market reports.

• An example

Perhaps an example may help to illustrate this point further. Let us consider conceived problems besetting British Airways. The company's passenger traffic has dropped on some routes, especially the North Atlantic routes, by as much as one-third. Now assume the question asks you to put yourself in the position of the Director of Strategy of BA and then make recommendations to the Chief Executive as to how the problems can be rectified. How do you go about it?

The first thing would be to collate suitable research that covers not only the airline itself but, more importantly, the industry as a whole and I mean the global airline industry not just the UK. During that task not only would you have found research articles that discuss the problem in detail, but you would also have found numerous articles that analyse and evaluate BA's financial and strategic position. These articles will also discuss where BA needs to go from here (i.e. what strategy options it has to reduce the extra capacity it is suffering and thus sustain its current profitability - if not increase it).

You will also have found research that discusses what BA's direct competitors (i.e. Virgin, United Airlines, American Airlines, etc.) have done as well as its indirect competitors (e.g. Easyjet, GO, Ryanair, etc.). For example, in response to the severe downturn in traffic as a result of, say, people's reluctance to board aircraft immediately after hijackings or terrorist attacks, the competitors might (as has happened in the past) immediately reduce fares to encourage passengers to carry on boarding planes. This is known as a 'cost reduction strategy' and has proved successful with the airlines implementing the strategy all reporting higher than average figures.

Consequently, this may well be a strategy you could recommend for BA, albeit a short-term one, until passenger confidence returns. You may also want to consider other cost-cutting strategies such as using smaller, more fuel-efficient aircraft, less frequent flights, staff and wage cutting measures, etc.

The key here is that, in sifting through the research information, you should come across various ideas that other companies have used as well as ideas that the people in the know (i.e. the experts) recommend. Simply build on these ideas and, before you know it, you will find that you have a long list of feasible and impressive recommendations.

In terms of theory, the best ones that spring to mind in this case, without going into too much detail, include a SWOT and PESTAL Analysis, use of the Boston (BGC) Matrix as well as a Value Chain Analysis. You may also want to use Porter's Five Forces Theory. Again, as each case will be different, your lecturer may be the best person to advise you on the best theories to employ, although he or she is unlikely to tell you how to relate them to the given case.

> **Remember:** With any assignment, in drawing on other people's hard work, always give them recognition by way of references. Put things into your own words and try to be original, as this impresses lecturers. Also, don't forget to state any reservations which apply to the recommendations which you have proposed as well as any assumptions you may have made.

14 ▶ Referencing and other areas

Including referencing (Harvard Style) throughout the text of your dissertation is only half the referencing requirement. The other half relates to the bibliography and reference list that you will need to assemble all at the end of the dissertation. Throughout the dissertation, you would have added condensed-references while at the end, you'll need to expand on these references so, for example, a reference in the dissertation may have read (Johnson, 1999) or (Branson, 2000). These would then need to be included at the back as:

1.   Johnson, P. 'The turbulence facing airlines' in The Journal for Airline Issues Vol.18 No.9 pp.45-61 (1999)

2.   Branson, R. 'Clouds in the impending skies for airlines' in Airline Business News. November 2000 p.31-32

3.   Ajuga, G. 'Will the world's airlines ever really take off?' in Flight International 18th of March 2001 p.13-14.

Supervisors like a long bibliography and reference list, as it shows that you have painstakingly gone through lots of books, newspapers, journals, etc. to produce the masterpiece in front of them. Luckily, you are allowed to list sources that you may have consulted in researching your dissertation but not necessarily included within it. Consequently, make sure you make the list as long as possible but within reason - of course.

15 ▶ And so - to conclude

In the above, I have guided you through all aspects of your dissertation from the moment you are notified of the requirement to write and submit one by your university to the compilation of all aspects of it. In doing so, I have taken you through the often-overlooked areas of the dissertation but areas which can mean the difference between a 2:1 and a 1:1 or 70% and 90%.

Don't forget that every university has its own specific layout and structure so you'll need to consult your university handbook to make sure that you write the dissertation applying the format specified by your university.

So I've told you how to assemble research as well as how to utilise fully the research into your assignment and/or dissertation. But what of obtaining the research? Where is the best places to go and more importantly, given that students have limited budgets, where are the cheapest places to go without compromising the quality of the research material? Don't be a "know the price of everything and the value of nothing" type of student. Life is not always about cost and besides, what is a few pounds when compared to getting a good, well-paid job? So "Read on" as the section after next deals with this special topic.

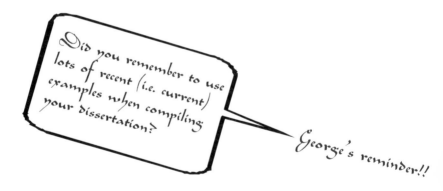

The final stage of a postgraduate (MBA/MSc/MA) programme is normally concerned with a written project of approximately 15,000 words in length. The project is intended to provide details of individual research into an agreed management issue. The project will normally be expected to contain an extended Executive Summary as well as more technical information relating to the study being undertaken.

What normally sets a postgraduate project apart from an undergraduate project is summarised by the following two factors: Firstly, the latter is usually approximately 10,000 words (5,000 words less than its counterpart) and secondly, the university would normally expect a postgraduate dissertation to be of a much higher quality. That is to say that the postgraduate dissertation will need to be of a much higher academic content.

Lastly, in going through this chapter of the practical guide, readers may find some of the areas somewhat repetitive of earlier sections. This has been done intentionally so as not to confuse readers who may wish to identify with each chapter in isolation.

 The Nature of Research

Research can be described as "finding out something you don't already know". However, such a very wide definition could include such activities as simply finding out the time of the next coach to Manchester - clearly not research that would be relevant to a postgraduate programme.

Alternatively, the collection of data to help determine, for example, what are the age, sex and occupations distribution of postgraduate students in Britain is useful information-gathering but perhaps little more than that. Such fact-gathering activities are often essential prior to establishing control mechanisms, policy formulation or decision-making but, for our purposes, they are not research!

Postgraduate research goes beyond fact-gathering, it requires analysis. It looks for explanations, relationships, comparisons, predictions, generalisations and theories. Such concepts are often typified by "why" questions. Why are there so few women postgraduate students? Why is the GNP in Britain increasing more slowly than in other countries?

These questions require effective information-gathering but also require the development of understanding - usually by comparisons, by relating to other factors and by creating and testing hypotheses. These are the characteristics of good postgraduate research.

The emphasis in most postgraduate projects will be upon problem-solving research. The problem has to be clearly defined and a method of solving it discovered. Often this will require consideration and application of a number of theories and concepts, usually ranging across several management disciplines.

 ## Selecting an Appropriate Project Topic

In selecting an appropriate topic you should consider identifying an area of work that is:

- Specifically interesting to you;

- Relevant to the development of your intended (for example - management) skills;

- Has value to your organisation (if appropriate).

It is anticipated that, in the majority of cases, the subject chosen for investigation will refer to a specific problem or opportunity that has some strategic significance. At this early stage, it may be appropriate only to identify a general management issue for investigation rather than provide a specific project title.

Whilst a project title is extremely important in helping any reader quickly understand the subject of the investigation, a more precisely-worded title may well develop as your research progresses.

3 ▶ Project Preparation

Perhaps the single most important aspect to assist you in preparing for the project is the need to plan in advance. There are three particular areas requiring consideration:

- Selecting a suitable topic (see above);

- Selecting an appropriate analytical framework (see below);

- The management of resources - particularly time.

The effective use of a project plan will help you to:

- Clarify your aims and objectives;

- Define the necessary activities and the order in which they should take place;

- Indicate critical points in the research in which progress can be reviewed and plans be assessed;

- Produce a time plan;

- Effectively use key resources;

- Define your priorities;

- Increase the likelihood of success.

George's Tip!!

Always use lots of recent (i.e. current) examples whenever possible when compiling your postgraduate dissertation.

4 ▶ Project Framework

A possible framework for your project is shown in tabular format on the following page:

Process	Notes
Terms of reference	Objectives:
	Clarification and negotiation
	Practical problem
	Multi-disciplinary
	Masters level
	Development opportunity
	Feasibility
	Hypothesis where appropriate
Obtaining collaboration and access	To appropriate problem area
	To data and people during the study
	To mentor
	To tutor
Search for other studies	Identification of existing knowledge relevant to project
	What others have done, review of literature
	Search within organisation
	Contact with other organisations
Determining methods	Starting assumptions.
	Project design
	Descriptive and predictive models. Networks, simulations etc.
Data collection	Historical analysis, statistical & comparative data
	Questionnaire, interviews, discussions, own experiences
Data Analysis	Validity, reliability, significance. Sources of error
	Evaluation process
	Establishing relationship
Conclusions and recommendations	Measuring effectiveness, setting standards
	Determining implications and proposing courses of action
Managing the implementation	Selling proposals, preparing the ground for changes, coping with resistance, political realities
Reflections	Reflecting on the learning and management development process of the project
Writing the thesis	

5 ▶ Project Proposal

This is the first formal stage of the project process. It usually involves the preparation of a detailed proposal, which will account for 15% of the total project mark.

The proposal is usually between 2,000 - 2,500 words. It needs to explain, in detail, the issue to be addressed, the reasons for choosing this issue and the broad methodological framework which will be adopted. In addition, it needs to specify, in detail, the data/ information, which will be used, where or how this will be obtained and the analytical techniques which will be appropriate given the issue and the information available.

A detailed timetable is also usually required as is evidence of a thorough literature search by the student and evaluation of the key articles relevant to your chosen topic.

To help all students successfully complete the Project Proposal the following framework is suggested, although it should be recognised that this may not be appropriate in all cases as each university's requirements differ.

Background and Overview

An introduction to the general area to be studied. The student will need to demonstrate his or her level of relevant theories and concepts based upon literature review. Evidence will need to be shown why the project's research is of importance.

Statement of Issue and Research Objectives

This is a listing of the detailed question(s) to be addressed along with the sponsoring organisation, target audience or mentor, as appropriate. The statement should contain an indication of why this detailed question is of particular importance, followed by a summary of what researching and reflecting upon this question is designed to achieve.

Methodology

Details of the approach to be adopted plus related management concepts should be accompanied by details of any information necessary to undertake the project and how this will be collected. For example: sources of primary data, sources of secondary data, outline of questionnaires, sampling method to be employed, structure of interviews, interviewees, instrument selection for qualitative data, etc.

In addition, you will need to outline any assumptions being made, constraints which you may face, and problems which could arise.

Analysis

Indicate clearly the technique or techniques to be used to analyse your information and how they will be used in the context of your particular project. If using quantitative analysis, explain in detail how the particular techniques will be used in conjunction with your eventual data set.

Structure of Final Project

Give preliminary ideas on the major chapters and sections to be included in the Final Project together with an outline of the material which is likely to be contained in each.

Time Schedule

Indicate the commencement dates and completion dates for all major activities, using a Gantt Chart (if possible) annexed to the proposal. Consider how you will manage the work of the project - what barriers there may be and how you will overcome them, what resources (time, people, equipment, etc.) you will bring to bear.

Preparing Draft Chapters

During the 'dead times' of any project (for example, whilst waiting for questionnaire responses), it is always worthwhile to write up, in draft format, any material that has already been collected. Introductory chapters can often be completed well before external data has been collected or analysed. The more of this draft material a tutor sees, the more useful feedback will be obtained.

Communications

Most university projects (undergraduate and postgraduate) are usually marked by the academic tutor and a second marker. Whilst tutors will have a good understanding of projects throughout the research period, second markers and external examiners will not. The project must effectively communicate to them the aims and achievements of the research process.

Limitations

Conclusions and recommendations will need to be drawn from the data as collected, analysed and presented in the project. They should be relevant to the aims of the project and will be limited by the scope of the research. You will be expected to examine data critically and not just present information as an attempt to justify any preconceived conclusions.

You will also need to be able to distinguish valid, from spurious, research.

 The Research Process

The Literature Survey

What sort of literature is likely to be relevant to any defined project and its objective(s)?

- in what discipline (management, psychology, sociology etc.)?
- in books, periodicals, company reports?
- unpublished?
- are they classic works or current thinking?

How do I undertake the literature research and acquire the relevant items?

- how shall I survey the literature?
- how many different surveys shall I carry out?
- how long will this take?
- how shall I know when to stop?

What am I looking for in the literature?

- what is the full extent of the ground?
- how much is relevant?
- are there any authorities in the field?
- what are the major findings overall?
- are any of particular relevance to this project?
- are there any significant omissions as far as this project is concerned?
- is it necessary to look elsewhere?
- what are the concepts and definitions commonly used?
- which of these should be adopted and why?
- what theories, models, conceptual frameworks are used?
- which of these are relevant to this project?
- what research methods are commonly used?
- are any of relevance to this project?
- is it necessary to read further in the literature on research methods?
- how will confidentiality be maintained?

Fieldwork

- What are the influences/constraints upon undertaking fieldwork:

    - in terms of the overall project schedule?

    - in terms of personal timetable availabilities?

    - in terms of respondents timetable availabilities?

- What time is needed/available to undertake the pilot study?

- How long will each interview require - for completion and for analysis? How long will the interviews or questionnaires be scheduled within the time available for the project?

- When will the fieldwork be undertaken - during the day or during the evening?

- What are the expected costs of photocopying, postage, travelling, tapes, etc?

- Who will bear these costs?

- Will special arrangements be required regarding the conduct of the interviews photocopying, postage etc?

- Will a preliminary letter of invitation/explanation/assurance of confidentiality to respondents be required?

- What will be provided to respondents in exchange for their time and cooperation? Some feedback? A copy of the final Project? Some other incentive! Or will participation be sufficient reward for them?

- Will the questions being asked generate anxiety or fear in your respondents? If so how will this be handled?

Analysis

- How detailed will the analysis be? Will all categories be covered from the material collected?

- Will tape-recorded interviews be transcribed? In whole or in part?

- How will spoilt or incomplete questionnaires be dealt with?
- How will respondents be identified or will they remain anonymous?
- Will quantitative or qualitative analysis be appropriate? Or both?
    - if quantitative, will correlation be looked for? What tests of significanoo will be appropriate?
    - if qualitative, will the weight or frequency of the replies require assessment? How will this be done? Will the method of data collection permit this?
    - if qualitative, how will something of particular significance be identified? Does the data collection method facilitate this?
    - if qualitative, how will associations between categories be identified? Does the system of data collection help this?
- How will individual quotations be identified, stored and retrieved?
- Will a spreadsheet be used or a computer package?
- What methods are to be used for identifying and keeping trace of aspects which need further investigation to complete the analysis?
- How can the results of the analysis above be understood? Are there any conceptual models in the literature which explain or illuminate them? Are there any organisational facts or situations which throw light on them?
- Are some of the results unexpected and not explicable as above? Can they be explained in some other way? Do they form a pattern which suggests a new conceptual model?
- Do the results meet the aims of the study? In what way and to what extent? Is further material required?
- What will be done if these results do not meet the aims or lack interest, significance or novelty or if they are far from clear-cut?

Conducting Interviews

Many researchers decide to use face-to-face interviews as an appropriate means of acquiring information. One advantage of interviewing is its adaptability. A skillful interviewer can follow up leads, probe responses, investigate motives and feelings which a questionnaire can never do. However, there are difficulties. It is a time-consuming and highly subjective technique so there is always a dangor of bias.

Wording the questions carefully, noting and analysing the responses, are demanding tasks.

Both interviews and questionnaires can heighten expectations of change within an organisation. If an interview has been conducted or a questionnaire has been circulated, staff will often expect management to respond to criticisms. This can also affect the subject's response. Care should be taken to explain quite clearly the purpose of any interview or questionnaire.

Before conducting interviews, consideration should be given to all of the following:

- has an appropriate sampling technique been used?

- do questions allow for a full response?

- are all responses noted (possibly using a tape-recorder)?

- avoid the possibility of 'interviewer bias' with the interviewer leading the respondent either consciously or subconsciously.

- is interviewing the right method?

- would questionnaires be better?

- would longer, better considered, written responses be more appropriate?

- can the responses be effectively analysed?

Designing Questionnaires

Questionnaires are probably the most common method of information collection. They are cheap to administer, can be sent to a large number of subjects and, provided they are well-designed, are relatively easy to analyse. Effective questionnaires are, however, difficult to design. Finding the right words, the best layout and the method of distribution most likely to yield a good response is skilled work. The following factors need to be considered:

Planning:

Structure the questionnaire to aid subsequent analysis. Decide the role of open-ended questions in advance. How will non-responses to some questions be handled?

Question structure:

How will questions be structured (dichotomous or multi-choice) or open questions or both? How will scaling techniques be used? Will ranking techniques be used? Will flash-card questions/choices be of use? Will incomprehensible jargon be avoided?

Questionnaire design:

How can the presentation of the questionnaire be improved? Can the questions be easily read (do not over photo-reduce). Is the layout consistent?

Are the questions in the appropriate order? Is the questionnaire over-long? Are all instructions unambiguous?

Is the respondent thanked and given clear instructions what to do with the completed questionnaire?

Purpose of Questionnaire:

Do your respondents know:

>> why the research is being undertaken?
>> what they gain as a result of completing your questionnaire?

Questionnaire testing:

Are the instructions, questions, analytical procedures and likely responses to be tested? Is it possible to test on sufficient, appropriate people? Will there be time to modify the research in the light of test results?

Distribution:

- By post or personal delivery?
- Will 'post paid' envelopes be included?
- Are there deadlines for responses?
- Is there an incentive to complete the questionnaire?
- Will all responses be identified, anonymous or optional?
- Will non-respondents be followed-up?

Client Relationships

Some projects will be organisation-based; hence, the relationship which is established between the researcher and the client organisation will be extremely important. In several respects, this relationship resembles that of consultant and client. The following information is aimed at maximising the opportunities that such a research project offer.

The 'consultant-client' relationship must be understood by both parties so as to achieve satisfactory results. This is likely to require the researcher being investigated and vice versa. A comparison of the client's definition of the project and the researcher's definition provides the basis of a sound working relationship, throughout the project. Such a comparison requires discussion.

It will be important to establish the boundaries of the research into the organisation. This will probably involve investigation into the organisation's resources including access to data and people. Confidentiality needs to be agreed - what is acceptable to the organisation and how extensive is the access to information?

In addition to the key 'contact' person in the client organisation, there may be further participants involved:

- liaison officers;

- employees doing work related to your project;

- managers and other employees who will be interviewed, asked to supply documents, consulted on various aspects of the project;

- managers and other employees who are not involved in the project but would like to know about it;

- managers and other employees who may be affected if the recommendations are implemented.

Relationships with all these people must be considered in advance and managed accordingly.

Access to information is a basic issue. If a client prevents your access to information, for whatever reason, and it is deemed that this information concerns the problems to be solved, the researcher must attempt to negotiate.

It must also be remembered that clients often forget to pass on information or consider it unimportant or unreliable although the researcher may have found it useful!

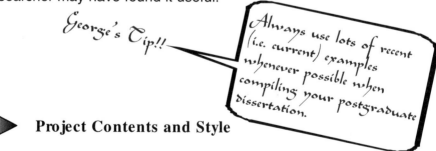

George's Tip!! — *Always use lots of recent (i.e. current) examples whenever possible when compiling your postgraduate dissertation.*

7 ▶ Project Contents and Style

A typical Project would include the items shown in the list on the following page:

Title Page

Contents List

Acknowledgements

Executive Summary

Introduction

Main Body (Chapters, Sections, etc.)

Conclusions

Recommendations

Reflections

References

Appendices

Title Page

The Project Title is important as it needs to indicate, quite clearly, what the project is about. It is useful, when considering a title, also to bear in mind how the work may be indexed and coded for information storage and retrieval purposes (what key words should the title incorporate). Abbreviations and specialist jargon should be avoided. Some projects will undoubtedly present information that either the sponsoring organisation or the researcher considers confidential and so, if this is the case, the title pages of all submitted work must be clearly marked 'CONFIDENTIAL'.

Contents List

A table of the various chapters and sections of the project must be included together with clear page references to each of these. Well documented contents will quickly show any reader the scope and direction of the work.

Executive Summary

The final project will need an extended Executive Summary which emphasises the main findings of the study. In particular, this Executive Summary will need to contain:

- an introduction telling the reader what the project is about, its objective;
- terms of reference and a description of the approach used;
- a summary of the information collected and analysis undertaken;
- details of the conclusions, recommendations and any action plans;
- detailed plans for implementing any recommended changes.

It is highly advisable that the Executive Summary only be written after the project is completed. It is often very difficult to write an effective summary as it should contain a complete overview of the whole project. It needs to provide an informative outline of contents, conclusions and recommendations of the project. There should also be some indications of the methods used. It must be presented in a coherent form - not as a list of headings or topics.

Introduction

An Introduction sets the scene putting the research into its context and explaining what led up to it. The Introduction is essential in order to tell the reader what the project is intended to provide - it is more than just the first section of the project. It should include a statement of the purpose or objectives of the inquiry, the terms of reference, the sources of information on which the project is based and how it was collected. The Introduction sets the scene and puts the whole inquiry into its proper context. It should explain why the research was carried out and outline the significance of related work on the topic. The Introduction may provide necessary background but only if it is relevant and brief. It may also inform the reader how the subject will be developed.

Main Body of the Project

This should commence with a clear explanation and definition of the topic or problem to be investigated including a statement of the management issues involved and how the topic and issues changed as the work evolved (including how any such changes are handled). It should also contain a review and appraisal of relevant previous work and a detailed account of the methodology used and why it was chosen (including details of any problems that were experienced).

It is likely that the main body of the project will contain several chapters/sections and subsections. All such divisions should be identified using a decimal notation system whereby major sections are given single numbers 1, 2, 3, and so on, in sequence. The first level of subsection will follow a decimal point, for example 1.1 and the first sub-subsection, under this subsection will repeat the process, that is 1.1.1, and so on. Be careful to avoid too many subsections as this will simply lead to confusion and reading difficulties.

The final part of the Main Body may be a summary of the discussion elements of the project, immediately prior to the project's Conclusions.

Conclusions

The Conclusions must be drawn from the body of evidence presented in the main sections of the project. Each separate conclusion should be acknowledged - possibly by numerical subsections.

The Conclusions should be seen to flow clearly from the preceding analysis and should also indicate any problems that had been identified and which will be the subject of recommended solutions.

Recommendations

This section will suggest ways of solving the problems, how the recommended courses of action will help to achieve the aims of the project, the benefits and cost of implementing the recommendations, the program of work that is required, the timescale involved and the resource implications. Recommendations should flow logically from the conclusions of the research - indeed they are sometimes combined under a joint heading.

Reflections

This section will contain an analysis and evaluation of the research process with, particularly, an assessment of the strengths and weaknesses of the project, any problems or constraints encountered during the project and how these difficulties were resolved. In addition, an evaluation of the effectiveness of the chosen methodology can be expected together with an assessment of how individual management competencies have been developed.

The following questions may be useful in providing a framework for this section:

- were the project objectives well-defined and fulfilled?
- how did the outcomes compare with initial expectations?
- was the research well-planned and executed?
- what went well and what would be done differently?
- how sensitive was the researcher to the abilities and contributions of others?
- what was learnt in terms of management experience and the development of specific management competencies?
- what would be your recommendations for improving the project in the light of your experiences.

References

References serve two purposes. They enable the reader to check information from external sources and to follow-up those sources if further information is required. References also acknowledge the debt of the reader to other writers who work has been used. References include all sources which have actually been referred to in the body of the project but do not include peripheral readings.

In order to identify, clearly and accurately, a particular source, it is necessary to have certain minimal information. This information primarily consists of the name of the author, the year of publication, the title of the publication, the place of publication and the name of the publisher. Further specific information is dependent upon the nature of the publication being referred to. There are a number of ways in which bibliographical data can be presented. It is important, however, that consistency in referencing is maintained by keeping to a single system.

One such system is described below and, although it appears to be complicated, it is remarkably simple to use once the habit of applying it has been acquired. The following examples illustrate the use of capital and lower case letters, punctuation marks and layout, all of which have a specific function.

The simplest reference form is that for books which have been published as single editions; examples are as follows:

ARNHEIM, R. (1956) Art Education: its Philosophy and Psychology. Indianapolis: Bobbs Merill.

GRAHAM, R. (1966) The Pickworth Fragment. Wymondham: Wymondham Press.

When books have been published in subsequent editions, it is important to specify the edition number as there are often considerable differences between editions. The edition number is shown in parenthesis after the title as shown in the following examples:

HALL, L. (1979) Business Administration (3rd edition). Estover, Plymouth: Macdonald and Evans.

LOWENFIELD, V. and BRITTAIN, L. (1970) Creative and Mental Growth (5th edition). New York: Collier Macmillan.

Publications which consist of collections of writing by a number of authors are identified under the names of the editors. Listings, indexes or collections of abstracts are similarly identified by the names of editors. The editors are designated by the abbreviations (Ed.) or (Eds.) after the name as shown below:

EISNER, E. W. & ECKER, D. W. (Eds.) (1966) Readings in Art Education. London: Ginn Blaisdel.

WEINSHALL, T. D. (Ed.) (1977) Culture and Management. Harmondsworth: Penguin.

References to specific chapters or articles in edited collections are identified under the names of the particular authors and then reference is made to the whole publication as above. It is, however, only the names of the particular authors which are capitalised. If the date when the specific chapter was originally published differs from that of the collected edition, it is necessary to include both dates. It is standard practice to give the page numbers of the article and, as the whole publication is the primary source of reference, it is the title of the whole publication which is underlined as shown in the following examples:

FAYERWEATHER, J. (1960) "Personal Relations" in Weinshall, T. D. (Ed.) (1977) Culture and Management. Harmondsworth: Penguin. pp107-135.

KAUFMAN, I. (1971) "The Art of Curriculum Making in the Arts" in Eisner, E. W. (Ed.) Confronting Curriculum Reform. Boston: Little Brown and Co.

Articles in periodicals are always the most difficult to locate so it is essential to have complete bibliographical data. The actual periodical in which an article appears is the major reference source and so it is the name of the periodical which is underlined. Most learned journals tend to have long titles and so, for bibliographic purposes, these are reduced to standardised abbreviations. Periodicals differ in the ways in which the different issues are designated but the most popular form is the attribution of a volume number which quite often relates to a particular year of publication and then an issue or part number within a volume. The numbers of the pages on which the article appears also needs to be given, as below:

FELDMAN, E. C. (1973) "The Teacher as Model Critic", Journal of Education. Vol. 7, No 1, pp2-17.

HANNIGAN, J. A. (1980) "Fragmentation in Science: The Case of Futurology", Sociology. Vol. 28, No 2, pp317-332.

Material which has not been published in the senses described above, such as Theses or Projects submitted for academic qualifications or papers read at conferences, require to be identified by the name of the material as well as the source or location as follows:

GRAHAM, R. (1974) The Casquets, Unpublished Paper. Second Annual Morison Lecture. Manchester Polytechnic.

HANCOCKS, M. (1973) Creativity in Education - A Selective Review of the Literature. Unpublished M.Sc. Thesis, Univ. of Bradford.

When compiling sources of reference, the entries are listed in alphabetical order of the names of the authors. If reference is made to more than one work by the same author, the entries are listed in chronological order of the dates of publication. When reference is made to more than one work by an author which were published in the same year, the works are differentiated by appending the letters a, b, c and so on to the year of publication, as in (1974a); (1974b); (1974c). References to the specific texts within the project, must necessarily maintain such designations.

Appendices

Appendices are essential in cases where a lot of detailed information exists which, if presented in the main body, would interrupt or spoil the flow of the project. Examples could be detailed tables of statistics, results of experiments, series of graphs etc. Remember that important items should be included in the text rather than requiring frequent reference to the appendices which can irritate readers. Appendices should be placed at the very end of the project and, if there is more than one, they should be clearly separated and labelled (for example: Appendix A, Appendix B, etc.) The appendices should be referred to at appropriate places in the text.

 8 ▶ Project Format

The front cover should be a title page, which must include the following information:

» The full title of the Project
» The full name of the Author
» The qualification for which the Project is submitted
» The month and year of submission.

A4-paper (210 mm x 297 mm) of good quality and sufficient opacity should be used with printing on only one side of the paper. A left-hand margin of ~25/40mm should be made available for binding - all other margins being 20mm. Line spacing of 1½ should be used for the typescript, except for indented quotations where single spacing may be used. Pages must be numbered consecutively throughout the text. Page numbers should be located centrally at the bottom of each page. Any abbreviations used should be those in normal use. Where necessary, a key to abbreviations should be provided.

These requirements must be adhered to. Beyond this, however, the exact format of the project is likely to vary according to the particular purpose and subject matter as well as your university's specific requirements. Remember, every little mark matters so don't lose valuable marks on what appear, at first sight, to be minor details!

 ## Assessment Criteria

Each Project will normally be assessed by a project supervisor and another tutor for second marking, before being passed to the external examiners. This process ensures that a consistent and appropriate standard of marking is being applied. Each university's marking criteria will usually differ but, generally speaking, assessment consideration will include the following:

General description of the Project

This should make it clear to the reader what the organisation involved does or, if the study is not organisation based, what the context of the inquiry is. There should be a definite statement of the purpose of the study. The topic or problem must be clearly explained and include an outline of what it is intended to achieve for the client organisation or target audience. Theories or conceptual frameworks guiding the work should be outlined and their application explained.

Methodology

The methodology used should be adequately explained and must be appropriate to the problem and the data. Reasons for using particular techniques should be explained. Data must be carefully collected and bias avoided. There should be evidence of a critical evaluation of sources of data. Data must be relevant and unimportant material should, of course, be excluded.

Analysis

The Project should demonstrate rigour in analysis of information taking an appropriate critical attitude. There should be a high standard of interpretative skills in analysing and understanding the results of the investigation.

The Literature

Relevant previous work should be reviewed and appraised. The project should demonstrate the ability to critically evaluate and make use of relevant sources.

Academic Content

Appropriate application of theories and concepts should be demonstrated. The student should show that they can relate theory to practice either to an organisational setting or to illuminate the managerial implications of a more general enquiry.

Conclusions and Recommendations

These should be based on the evidence and be clearly derived from the preceding analysis. Practical effectiveness and sensitivity should be shown in conclusions and recommendations with realistic awareness of constraints, where appropriate. Costs and benefits of recommendations should be quantified wherever practicable. Action plans should be well thought out and practicable.

The Lessons Learned

The project should discuss what the student has learned about the application both of concepts and techniques in carrying out the project. This should include an appraisal of research and management competencies enhanced, reflections on successes or failures, more general lessons of interest, and any areas identified as needing further investigation. This section should demonstrate a high standard of realism and sophistication, a developed awareness and understanding of the business setting and contain a genuinely thoughtful and well-considered critique.

Presentation

The project should be written in good English and be well presented with appropriate use and quality of graphics and illustrations. It should be well-structured with clear and explanatory section headings. The sections of each part of the project should be clear and logical and hang together particularly well. Projects should be correct in terms of the mechanics i.e. typing, spelling, grammar, tables, references, etc.

George's reminder!!

Did you remember to use lots of recent (i.e. current) examples when compiling your postgraduate dissertation?

Information Sources

In my experience, I have found there to be an unlimited number of sources from which a student can obtain quality research. However, in the interests of minimising costs whilst simultaneously ensuring that the quality of the research you obtain is of the highest quality, I have listed the institutes, libraries and websites that I feel should be more than adequate for the majority of assignments and/or dissertations. I have also taken the liberty to enclose the best search onginoε to uεe when looking for reεearch online.

Academic Research Institutes

These have been listed first, as I've found them to be by far the most effective and provide the easiest way of obtaining quality, yet affordable, academic research material. They all have an abundance of books, journal articles, magazines, and other serial titles suitable for your research needs. Additionally, they have research assistants who specialise in catering for your every need and who are at hand to assist in your endeavours.

The only downside to these institutes are that they charge for membership although, to their credit, students are given membership discounts without limiting access to all their research material. Another important thing to look out for with research institutes is that they charge between £3 to £4 per article if they carry out the research for you but, a little known fact is that if you can be bothered to attend and do the research yourself, which entails picking out the journals from the library and photocopying them yourself, the cost becomes as little as 0.15p per page.

» The Chartered Institute of Personnel & Development (CIPD)

Address: Camp House, Camp Road, Wimbledon SW19 4UX.

The CIPD library caters for research in the areas of Occupational Psychology, Human Resource Management, Business Management, Employment Law and all other areas pertaining to the workplace. The library is well laid out and so locating the articles is very easy indeed. The yearly membership fee of £149, which may seem expensive, is well worth it considering the wealth of research in the library.

Getting research

The library can carry out the research on your behalf although this may prove expensive at £4.00 per article (irrespective of length). A better option, depending on how far you live from the institute, would be to go there in person and carry out the research yourself. Doing things this way will cost you no more than 0.15p per page in photocopying. The research staff will be more than glad to give you a reading list of articles upon you presenting them with the area(s) you want to research. The maximum number of books that can be borrowed at any one time is four.

Membership fee: £149 pa.

Contact Number (direct to library): 020-8263-3355

Website: www.cipd.co.uk

Downside: The membership fee.

Star Rating: ★★★★★

» The Institute of Management (IOM)

Address: Management Information Centre, Management House, Cottingham Road, Corby, Northants. NN17 1TT.

The IOM caters for research pertaining mostly to the area of business and management related subjects. It does have articles in other areas and their availability is dependent on the subject you have chosen to research.

Getting research

Unlike its counterparts, although the IOM gives members the option of either coming to the Institute and carrying out research themselves or having it sent to your address, the fee of £4.00 per article remains the same. Consequently, you will be better-off letting them do all the work for you. Having joined the Institute and when making a research enquiry, your phone call will result in a research assistant taking the necessary details of your research topic(s).

Having processed this, the IOM will either email you (same day depending on time ordered) or send you a reading list (usually next day) along with an ordering (copyright) form to be filled in for each article to be ordered. Note: There is no requirement to carry out such a time-consuming task for data from the CIPD (see above) nor the HCIMA (see below).

Upon filling-out and sending the forms back along with a cheque or faxing through your order along with your credit card details, the research usually arrives the next day. Non-members pay a fee of £6.00 per article. Maximum number of books that can be borrowed at any time is five.

Membership fee: £35 and £60 for F/T and P/T students, respectively

Contact Number: 01536-204222

Website: www.inst-mgt.org.uk

Downside: No photocopying concessions for making the effort to attend the Institute in person.

Star Rating: ★★★★

» The Chartered Institute of Marketing (CIM)

Address: Moor Hall, Cookham, Maidenhead, Berkshire SL6 9QH.

The CIM library specialises in all things marketing and is a 'must visit' place for all students doing marketing-related modules. The library is well laid out and all the research journals and books are easy to find. This, coupled with extremely helpful research assistants, makes the CIM library an ideal place to obtain marketing, business and management research. Naturally, the only downside is its location and unless you reside in that part of the country, travelling there can be tiresome.

Getting the research

Upon visiting or phoning the library, a research assistant will enter your research topic(s) into the library database and give you a research reading list of books and/or journals. This reading list will allow you to select the journals and books you want from the shelves. Alternatively, they can be sent to you should you choose to order over the phone. To photocopy articles costs 15p/page if you photocopy your own articles whilst, if they do it on your behalf, the fee is £4.00 per article.

Membership Fee: £121 for students

Contact Number: 01628-427500

Website: www.cim.co.uk

Downside: High cost of joining and location although, given its size, this is understandable.

Star Rating: ★★★★★

» Hotel and Catering International Management Association

Address: 191 Trinity Road, London SW17 7HN.

The HCIMA, as the name suggests, specialises in subjects relating to Hospitality and Tourism. The Association is well-equipped with books, journals and other articles for students studying any of the above subjects. Unlike the other institutes, it is not as well equipped or as big but the staff are helpful and always try to make your visit as enjoyable as possible.

Getting the research

When visiting the Association personally, a research assistant will help you obtain a reading list of articles. The charge for carrying out the research yourself is 10p/page. You are advised to get there very early as the library (which is small) does become crowded with other students towards the afternoon. The other option open to you is to request the articles over the phone upon which you'll be charged £2.00 per article.

Membership Fees (examples)

> Joining between 1st September and 30th November: £30 pays for membership until the 30th November (the following year).

> Joining between 1st December and 31st March (the following year): £30 pays for membership until the 30th November (in the following year).

> Joining between 1st April and 31st August: £15 pays for membership until 30th November (in the same year).

Contact: 020-8772-7400

Website: www.hcima.co.uk

Downside: The library is very small with only one public photocopier. If you get there in the afternoon, the staff will not have re-shelved the articles that other students to the library may have left out earlier. Consequently, when attempting to pick out your journals, don't be surprised if some of them are not in their folders - this can be very frustrating, especially if you're pushed for time!

Star rating: ★★★

» Libraries (in the London area)

I have found three very good libraries in the London area, although I recognise that this information may be of little use to students studying outside of London.

• The University of London Library - Senate House (Psychology)

This library is very well-equipped so I have chosen to include it in my list for the benefit of students studying psychology. The library has a psychology database, which enables students to search for associated journals going back years. Upon getting a reading list (yourself), the library is well-equipped with the relevant journals to enable you to photocopy them. Students get in *free* whilst there is a membership fee for non-students.

- **Croydon Central Library, Katherine Street, Croydon**

This library has been given a mention for two special reasons. Firstly, it is the only place I know that allows you to download an entire market report with no restrictions whatsoever. In other places, you are only allowed to photocopy 5 to 10% of the report. This library usually has two market report companies on its database: Mintel and Market Assessment Publications (MAPs).

Secondly, the library has an extremely good database of CD-ROM articles including FT McCarthy going back at least five years. Printing costs 20p per page and the Central Library in Croydon is well worth a visit if your university library's database is lacking.

Contact: 020-8760-5400

- **The City of London Business Library**

Situated in the City of London close to Moorgate Underground Station, this is an ideal library for students studying business-related subjects.

 Internet Research

Students are attempting, increasingly, to obtain academic research via the Internet. Personally, I am somewhat sceptical about the capabilities of this medium to provide quality academic research free-of-charge.

However, I have found the Internet to be suitable for obtaining specific pieces of information for assignments and dissertations such as company information, newspaper articles and occasionally (if you're lucky) quality and (free) academic articles.

In spite of my earlier (guarded) statement about the use of the Internet, I can reveal that there are sites where you will be able to download quality academic journals absolutely free of charge. But, as any keen surfer will tell you, the quality of information you find is dependent on three key factors: the search engine used, the quality of your Internet connection (i.e. modem, leased line, etc.) and, most of all, your patience.

» Search engines

Having spent hour-upon-hour searching the Internet for various pieces of research, I have employed the use of all the major search engines. In doing so, two search engines have stood out in delivering quality and relevant information time-after-time. They are namely:

Google - www.google.com

Metacrawler - www.metacrawler.com

I think you will find these two search engines to be not only quick, but more importantly, adept at bringing up relevant information time-after-time. Naturally, like all search engines, you'll have to sift through a lot of extraneous material but, if you persevere, I guarantee that you'll come across a lot of quality and relevant articles for your assignment and/or dissertation.

» Relevant sites to visit for academic research material

In my years of compiling assignments, I have built up my own mental list of useful academic research websites where students can download whole journals. Some of the sites (depending on the articles) will allow you to download an entire article free-of-charge while others may charge a nominal fee.

My list is shown on the following page:

My short list of recommended websites:

- www.elsevier.nl
- www.sagepub.com
- mcb.co.uk
- burkeinstitute.com
- emerald-library.com
- www.law.duke.edu
- www.indiana.edu
- www.papers.ssrn.com

Help & Advice

In writing this practical guide, I have attempted to cover all possible angles and scenarios. Naturally, every assignment/dissertation is different and will, at times, need specific guidance.

Consequently, I would recommend that, should you require any further assistance for your particular assignment and/or dissertation, or if you have any question whatsoever about any area covered in this guide, then please telephone my recommended student advice, guidance and support hotline, the number for which is given on the Just4students.com website:

For FREE general assignment/dissertation advice from the author of this practical guide, please contact him via email at:

george@mailrun.co.uk

All callers please note that due to the volume of emails, please allow at least three working days for a response. Also please note that the author will only entertain email queries from (and reply to) mailrun account holders. If you haven't got an account, you may obtain one FREE at:

www.mailrun.co.uk

For your copy of a sample assignment*, to use as a reference in association with this practical guide as well as for clarification purposes, please send a cheque for only £4.99 (inc.P&P) - payable to Just4students Ltd. - to Just4students Ltd., 8 The High Parade, Parade House, Streatham High Road, London SW16 1EX. Please remember to include your name and address with your order and cheque (Delivery within seven days).

* The sample assignment is entitled: *"Global firms that employ a cultural diverse workforce within their management structure can derive a competitive advantage within their respective industries. Discuss."*

Useful Research Addresses & Phone Numbers

(Students please note that addresses and phone numbers may have changed since
going to press)

Just4students.com – for research in Management, HRM,
Marketing, Law, Tourism, Hospitality, Occupational
Pyschology, and other general areas.   www.just4students.com

Chartered Institute of Management Accountants in England and Wales,
Portland Place, London W1   0207 637 2311

Chartered Institute of Marketing,
Moor Hall, The Moor, Cookham   01628 524922

Chartered Institute of Patent Agents,
Staple Inn Buildings, London WC1   0207 405 9450

Chartered Institute of Purchasing and Supply,
Easton House, Easton-on-the-Hill, Stamford,   01780 756777

Chartered Institute of Taxation,
12 Upper Belgrave Street. London SW1   0207 235 9381

Chartered Institute of Transport,
80 Portland Place, London   0207 467 9400

Chartered Institute of Building Services Engineers,
222 Balham High Road, London SW12   0208 675 5211

Chartered Institute of Water and Environmental Management,
15 John Street, London WC1   0207 831 3110

Chartered Insurance Institute,
20 Aldermanbury, London EC2   0207 606 3835

Chartered Practice, The Architects,
159 Askew Road, London W12   0208 743 9535

Chartered Society of Designers,
32 Saffron Hill, London EC1,   0207 831 9777

Chartered Society of Physiotherapy,
14 Bedford Row, London WC1   0207 242 1941

Institute for African Alternatives,
Lyndhurst Hall, Warden Road, London NW5   0207 482 4660

Institute for Arts in Therapy and Education,
15 Windsor Street, London N1   0207 704 2534

Institute for Complimentary Medicine,
PO Box 194, London SE16   0207 237 5165

Institute for Constitutional Research,
104 Kennington Road, London SE11   0207 793 0063

Institute for European Environmental Policy,
52 Horseferry Road, London SW1   0207 799 2244

Institute for Fiscal Studies,
7 Ridgmount Street, London WC1   0207 636 3784

Institute for Global Ethics,
17 Nottingham Street, London W1   0207 486 1954

Institute for Health Sector Development,
27 Old Street, London EC1   0207 253 2222

Institute for International Communication,
56 Eccleston Square, London SW1   0207 233 9888

Institute for Jewish Policy Research, 79 Wimpole Street, London W1	**0207 935 8266**
Institute for Manufacturing, 24 Buckingham Gate, London SW1	**0207 828 8878**
Institute for Policy Research, Grosvenor Garden House, Grosvenor Gardens, London SW1	**0207 828 6626**
Institute for Public Policy Research, 30 Southampton Street, London WC2	**0207 470 6100**
Institute for Scientific Information, Brunel Science Park, Kingston Lane, Uxbridge	**01895 270016**
Institute for Social Inventions, 20 Heber Road, London NW2	**0208 208 2853**
Institute for Study Abroad, 21 Pembridge Gardens, London W2	**0207 792 8751**
Institute for Study of Political Power, 8 Willow Road, London NW3	**0207 794 8717**
Institute for the Study of Drug Dependence, 32 Loman Street, London SE1	**0207 803 4720**
Institute for War and Peace Reporting, 31 Islington High Street, London N1	**0207 713 7130**
Institute Jozef Pilsudski, Science Institute, 238 King Street, London W6	**0208 748 6197**
Institute of Acoustics Ltd., 77a St Peter's Street, St Albans	**01727 848195**
Institute of Actuaries, Staple Inn Hall, Staple Inn, London WC1	**0207 632 2100**
Institute of Advanced Legal Studies, University of London, 17 Russell Square, London	**0207 637 1731**
Institute of Alcohol Studies, 12 Caxton Street, London SW1	**0207 222 5880**
Institute of Archaeology, University College London, Gower Street, London WC1	**0207 887 7050**
Institute of Barristers Clerks, 4 Essex Court, Temple, London EC4	**0207 353 2699**
Institute of Biology, 20 Queensbury Place, London SW7	**0207 581 8333**
Institute of Biomedical Science, 12 Coldbath Square, London EC1	**0207 837 3286**
Institute of Brewing, 33 Clarges Street, London W1	**0207 499 8144**
Institute of British Organ Building, 49 Chelmsford Road, London E18	**0208 559 7477**
Institute of Broadcast Sound, The Old Orchard, Blancahrds Hill, Guildford	**01483 575450**
Institute of Business Ethics, 24 Greencoat Place, London SW1	**0207 798 6040**
Institute of Business Psychology, 8 Willow Road, London NW3	**0207 794 8717**
Institute of Risk Management, 8 Lloyds Avenue, London EC3	**0207 709 9808**
Institute of Road Transport Engineers, 22 Greencoat Place, London SW1	**0207 630 1111**

Institute of Roofing, 24 Weymouth Street, London W1	**0207 436 0103**
Institute of Sales Promotions, 66 Pentonville Road, London N1	**0207 278 3058**
Institute of Samurai Strategy, 8 Willow Road, London NW3	**0207 794 8717**
Institute of Small Business Management, 21Woodrange Road, London E7	**0208 519 4107**
Institute of Social & Ethical Accountability, 44 Southwark Street, London SE1	**0207 407 7370**
Institute of Sport Psychology, 8 Willow Road, London NW3	**0207 794 8717**
Institute of Sports Sponsorship, Francis House, Francis Street, London SW1	**0207 233 7747**
Institute of Team Psychology, 8 Willow Road, London NW3	**0207 794 8717**
Institute of Technology and Research, 213 Borough High Street, London SE1	**0207 407 2078**
Institute of Translation & Interpreting, 377 City Road, London EC1	**0207 713 7600**
Institute of Zoology, Zoological Society of London, Regents Park, London NW1	**0207 722 3333**
Institute of Analysts and Programmers, 36 Culmington Road, London W13	**0208 567 2118**
Institute of British Engineers, 6 Hampton Place, Brighton	**01273 734274**
Institute of Chartered Surveyors, Royal, 12 Great George Street, London SW1	**0207 222 7000**
Institution of Chemical Engineers, 12 Gayfere Street, London SW1	**0207 222 2681**
Institution of Civil Engineers, Great George Street, London SW1	**0207 222 7722**
Institution of Electrical Engineers, 2 Savoy Place, London WC2	**0207 240 1871**
Institution of Environmental Sciences, 14 Princes Gate, London SW7	**01778 394846**
Institution of Highways Transportation, 6 Endsleigh Street, London WC1	**0207 387 2525**
Institution of Medical Engineers, 1 Birdcage Walk, London SW1	**0207 222 7899**
Institution of Mining & Metallurgy, 77 Hallam Street, London W1	**0207 580 3802**
Institution of Nuclear Engineers, 1 Penerley Road, London SE6	**0208 698 1500**
Institution of Plant Engineers, 77 Great Peter Street, London SW1	**0207 233 2855**
Institution of Railway Signal Engineers, Savoy Hill House, Savoy Hill, London WC2	**0207 240 3290**
Institute of Structural Engineers, 11 Upper Belgrave Street, London SW1	**0207 235 4535**